Guided Meditation Scripts for Wellness Professionals

Mindfulness, Breathwork, and Relaxation for Yoga Teachers, Coaches, Therapists, and Holistic Practitioners

Ava Redfern

Table of Contents

Introduction

For a professional, few things are more rewarding than making a meaningful impact in someone's life, whether a student, a client, or something in between. These are people seeking relief from the relentless pressures of modern existence—pressures that pull them away from themselves and leave them feeling unbalanced.

Think of the people you work with on a regular basis and imagine handing each of them a key—not a physical key but a practice that unlocks the door to inner peace, comfort, and growth. This book is here to equip you with that very key: the power of mindfulness and meditation practices explicitly tailored for yoga teachers, life coaches, therapists, counselors, and holistic practitioners. This means discovering new dimensions in your role as a guide, facilitator, and healer. Whether you're looking to diversify your teaching methods with mindfulness techniques or enrich coaching sessions and therapy with grounding practices, this book promises growth and greatness not only for those you serve but also for you as a practitioner.

Our goal here is clear: By the end, you'll not only be empowered to integrate mindfulness and meditation techniques seamlessly into your work, but you'll also learn to tailor these practices to meet the unique needs of your students, clients, and patients. The pages ahead will show you various key pieces of information, as well as more than 100 meditation scripts that can help alleviate stress and anxiety, promoting emotional well-being and holistic growth. When shared with those you work with, these resources offer incredible benefits for fulfillment and emotional stability. Each chapter is carefully crafted to build on the last.

How to Use This Book

This book is meant to be your tool; you can use it however you please. It is packed with actionable advice and meditation scripts that cover a wide range of topics, including:

- The foundations of meditation—a quick refresher on core concepts and what makes these meditations particularly effective.

- Short scripts perfect for quick calming sessions where someone you work with needs a moment of peace.

- Moderate-length scripts that help improve stamina with meditation and encourage clients, students, and others to engage with meditation for a more substantial amount of time.

- Extended scripts to improve and fortify meditation-based growth.

- Scripts that tie breathwork into meditation for a more fulfilling practice.

- Specific practices for resilience and emotional well-being.

- And many more!

That said, you don't have to follow any strict rules for this book. Take what you want and leave what you don't want. If that means reading scripts directly to those you work with, tailoring a plan based on the variety of scripts available, or even adapting them to suit your style more effectively, take the initiative and make it work for you.

So, ready yourself and those you work with. Align your intentions and take a deep, conscious breath. Together, we'll navigate the resources you need to take meditation to the next level for those you work with. Thank you for stepping onto this path—one where the destination promises not only a better understanding of your role in others' lives but a newfound perspective on the journey to peace.

Chapter 1:

Foundation of Mindfulness and

Meditation

Mindfulness and meditation, as you know, are practices with roots deeply embedded in the pursuit of mental, emotional, and physical well-being. For wellness professionals, these practices help build deeper connections with clients while simultaneously promoting personal growth. This chapter will serve as a refresher on these concepts, shedding light on how they can enhance both your professional practice and personal life.

Understanding and Applying Mindfulness

Mindfulness is a concept that describes being fully present in the current moment, specifically through non-judgmental awareness of your thoughts, feelings, and bodily sensations (Mindful Staff, 2020). This concept may sound simple, yet it holds profound implications for both wellness professionals and their clients. For yoga teachers, life coaches, therapists, counselors, and holistic practitioners, integrating mindfulness can yield incredible results.

The power of mindfulness lies in its ability to enhance emotional awareness and improve communication. When practitioners are fully present, they become more attuned to the subtleties of their own feelings and those of their clients. This heightened emotional awareness fosters an environment where deeper understanding and empathy can flourish.

Beyond that, mindfulness has been shown to significantly reduce stress. Through mindful breathing and grounding exercises, professionals and clients can better regulate their emotions. This reduction in stress not only benefits the individual but also enriches therapeutic relationships. In this setting, clients feel safer and more understood, which can accelerate their progress and deepen their trust in the process ("Mindfulness Therapy," 2024).

Furthermore, mindfulness techniques can be readily adapted to suit diverse client needs, which enhances wellness sessions across various disciplines. Short exercises, such as the STOP technique—Stop, Take a breath, Observe, and Proceed—offer practical tools that practitioners can easily incorporate into sessions. These brief moments of mindfulness can break up tension and refocus energy, making each session more dynamic and responsive to the client's immediate state.

Scientific Framework of Meditation

Meditation has been increasingly recognized as an effective tool for enhancing wellness, particularly in professional settings such as yoga classes, life coaching, therapy, and holistic practices. This practice nurtures mental and emotional well-being and is also grounded in robust scientific principles that support its effectiveness. One key aspect of meditation is its ability to regulate cortisol levels, the hormone associated with stress (Fell, 2013).

Scientific studies have further shown that consistent meditation leads to increased gray matter in brain regions responsible for emotional regulation, particularly the prefrontal cortex and the right anterior insula (Hölzel et al., 2011). Also, mindfulness-based practices like meditation have been shown to stimulate changes in brain areas linked to attention and mood regulation, contributing to overall psychological well-being (Hölzel et al., 2011).

Another significant advantage of meditation lies in its effectiveness in decreasing symptoms of anxiety and depressive disorders. People engaged in regular meditation often report an improved ability to manage their moods and experience fewer episodes of anxiety and depression. Regular engagement in meditation develops a mindset better equipped to handle life's challenges, leading to a positive outlook and improved mental health.

Empirical research and meta-analyses have consistently affirmed the role of meditation as a reliable mental health intervention. Compared to traditional approaches, meditation offers unique advantages due to its simplicity and accessibility. A review of controlled studies shows that mindfulness-oriented interventions, such as mindfulness-based stress reduction (MBSR), have been beneficial in improving psychological health outcomes (Kriakous et al., 2021). Unlike many conventional treatments, meditation does not require any equipment or medication, making it a cost-effective and sustainable option for long-term mental health management.

Importantly, as meditation becomes more widely accepted and utilized within therapeutic and wellness contexts, ongoing research continues to uncover new insights into its mechanisms and benefits. Although existing evidence firmly establishes the value of meditation, further studies are necessary to fully understand the pathways through which it influences psychological and physiological processes. As our comprehension deepens, so too will the ways in which meditation can be tailored and adapted to meet diverse needs across different population groups.

Clarifying Meditation Misconceptions

Debunking the myths that shroud meditation is necessary, as there are many misconceptions surrounding meditation and mindfulness practices.

The first widespread misconception is the belief that meditation requires emptying the mind of all thoughts. This notion can be intimidating and discouraging for beginners and seasoned practitioners alike. Instead, meditation is a matter of observing one's thoughts without judgment or attachment.

Another important clarification is that meditation is far from being solely a religious or spiritual practice. While it indeed has roots in spiritual traditions, meditation today is widely practiced in secular contexts. This universality makes meditation a valuable tool for people from all walks of life.

It's also a prevalent myth that long hours of meditation are required to experience any tangible benefits. In reality, there is significant evidence that even brief meditation sessions can lead to immediate relaxation and mental clarity. You don't need to spend hours sitting cross-legged to feel calmer and more focused; just taking a few minutes daily can significantly impact your overall well-being.

Overall, adaptability is key to integrating meditation into diverse settings and for varied client needs. Techniques can be modified to suit different preferences and environments. Understanding and busting these myths means you can better guide your clients or students toward beneficial practices tailored to individual needs.

Intention Setting and Environment

Setting intentions is an important part of mindfulness and meditation practices, particularly for wellness professionals who aim to bring positive, uplifting experiences to their clients. Intentions provide direction and purpose during practice, which makes each session more impactful by aligning with personal values.

A significant part of setting effective intentions is the process itself. It requires specificity—knowing precisely what you aim to cultivate or achieve during your meditation or mindfulness sessions. Writing down these intentions can solidify them by putting them into more tangible terms on paper, and for many practices, simply thinking an intention to oneself can be just as meaningful. Discussing these intentions with clients provides them with a clearer understanding of the session's objectives and builds a collaborative atmosphere where both practitioner and client can reflect on progress and outcomes together.

Practical steps for setting clear intentions start by identifying what you want to focus on, and helping your client or student consider what they want their focus to be for a session or set of sessions. This could be improving patience, reducing stress, or elevating self-awareness. Once the intention is identified, writing it down or thinking it assertively helps to reinforce its significance. When your client shares these intentions, especially in a professional setting, it opens up dialogue about expectations and goals, which in turn reinforces commitment to the practice.

Intention-setting also plays a major part in motivation. When practitioners and clients set intentions, they establish a point for reflection, allowing both to look back on where they started and see how far they've come. This reflective practice can highlight personal growth and bring to light progress that might otherwise go unnoticed. Encouraging those you work with to set intentions will help keep them motivated, especially as you create a safe, collaborative space where they can share those intentions with you.

Creating a Strong Meditation Environment

Creating a conducive environment for meditation is non-negotiable. The surroundings in which meditation takes place can significantly influence its effectiveness. A supportive environment is clean and uncluttered, helping to avoid distractions and encourage a sense of calm and focus. Cleanliness here doesn't just refer to physical tidiness but also the absence of visual clutter, which can help transport practitioners into a meditative state more readily.

Sound considerations should also be kept in mind when creating a conducive meditation space. The auditory environment should be tranquil, whether it's silence, nature sounds, or soft background music. These sounds—or lack thereof—should encourage relaxation and deep focus. It's important to adjust sound levels according to the personal preference of those you work with in order to ensure it supports rather than hinders the practice.

Comfort aids are another aspect of creating a supportive meditation environment. This includes having comfortable seating or cushions, appropriate lighting, and personal items like cushions or blankets that enhance physical comfort. Comfort ensures that the physical body isn't a source of distraction and that the mind can focus solely on the meditative experience. Adjustments such as these acknowledge the individual needs of each client, contributing to a personalized and adaptable meditation practice.

Bringing It All Together

Mindfulness and meditation are ways of nurturing a more connected and fulfilling approach to wellness. The integration of mindfulness practices can reduce stress and create a supportive atmosphere for healing, leading to more positive interactions with those you work with and personal growth for each person whom you help. Whether you're guiding yoga students to focus on their breath or helping life coaching clients stay centered on their goals, these practices offer incredible benefits. Therapists and holistic practitioners can incorporate mindfulness to aid clients in developing resilience against stress and anxiety while creating a calm and focused environment. Each of these basics we've covered is helpful to integrate into your work—they can structure sessions and encourage stronger results for each student, client, or other person you help.

Chapter 2:

Short Guided Sessions for Quick

Calming

Short guided sessions for quick calming are becoming a popular way to maintain peace and balance in the middle of busy lives. Finding those precious few minutes to reset can feel like a small victory against the chaos of everyday stress, which is why short guided sessions are great to share with those you work with.

In this chapter, you'll discover various scripts designed specifically for quick relaxation and stress relief through brief meditation sessions. You'll get insights into different mindfulness techniques that can be seamlessly integrated into yoga classes, coaching sessions, or therapy settings to make your work more meaningful for yourself and others. Each method provides straightforward guidance so that even beginners you assist can benefit from these practices. As you read on, you'll gain the confidence to use these tools to enrich both personal and professional environments, creating spaces where peace and clarity can grow.

Five-Minute Mindfulness Reset

Mindfulness is gaining recognition for its impact on reducing anxiety and stress, which makes it a perfect tool for those seeking quick grounding techniques. Regular mindfulness practices can significantly improve mental well-being by curbing stress and fostering a sense of balance.

Script #1: Five-Minute Reconnect

Let's delve into a simple yet effective step-by-step mindfulness reset you can share to help your clients, students, or others center their thoughts and release distractions.

1. Take a moment to find a quiet, comfortable position. You may choose to sit or lie down, whatever feels best for you. When you're ready, allow your eyes to gently close or soften your gaze.

2. Bring your awareness to your breath. Take a deep inhale through your nose... and a slow, steady exhale through your mouth. Let your breath settle into its natural rhythm, effortless and smooth.

3. Notice the sensation of air flowing in... cool as it enters your nose... filling your lungs... and warm as it leaves through your mouth. There's nothing to change, nothing to force—just observing, just being.

4. (Pause for a few moments.)

5. If your mind begins to wander, gently guide your attention back to your breath, like returning home. Feel the rise and fall of your chest... the gentle support of the surface beneath you... the warmth of your breath moving through you. If you notice any areas of tension—perhaps in your shoulders, jaw, or hands—invite them to soften, to release.

6. Allow yourself to simply rest here, fully present. Thoughts may come and go like waves on the shore. Acknowledge them, and then return to the steady rhythm of your breath.

7. (Pause for 2-3 minutes, allowing space for deep relaxation.)

8. Take one more deep, intentional inhale... and a slow, complete exhale. And when you're ready, open your eyes, returning to this moment, refreshed and present.

Script #2: Five-Minute Stress Release

The next script I have for you is meant to help reduce tension through a five-minute mindfulness exercise. You can read this script directly to those you work with.

1. This short mindfulness exercise is designed to help you release tension and bring a sense of ease to your body and mind. Let's begin by finding a comfortable position—sitting or lying down—and allowing yourself to settle into stillness.

2. Gently close your eyes or soften your gaze. Take a slow, deep breath in through your nose... and exhale fully through your mouth. With each breath, feel your body becoming a little heavier, grounding into the surface beneath you.

3. (Pause for a few moments.)

4. Now, bring your awareness to your body, starting at the top of your head. Notice any areas of tightness or discomfort. Gently scan down through your face, neck, shoulders, arms, and hands—simply noticing without judgment. Continue this awareness down through your chest, back, hips, legs, and feet. If you find tension, imagine breathing into that space, softening with each exhale.

5. With every inhale, invite in relaxation. With every exhale, imagine letting go of tension. Picture it dissolving like mist, leaving your body lighter and more at ease.

6. (Pause for 2-3 minutes.)

7. Now, allow yourself to simply be. No need to change anything—just rest in this moment of presence, letting the breath flow naturally. If thoughts arise, acknowledge them and gently return to your breath.

8. (Pause for a few moments.)

9. When you're ready, take one more deep breath in... and slowly exhale. Begin to gently bring awareness back to your surroundings. When you feel ready, open your eyes. Carry this sense of ease with you as you continue your day.

Application in Practice

Integrating mindfulness into various settings is beneficial for enhancing both personal and professional experiences. Yoga classes are ideal for incorporating mindfulness, as they naturally combine physical movements with conscious breathing. Encourage your students or clients to bring mindful awareness to each posture, feeling the stretch and strength in their muscles while maintaining steady breaths. This conscientious approach to yoga enhances flexibility and creates a deeper connection with one's body and emotions, promoting relaxation and mental clarity.

For those you work with who are facing high-stress situations, such as during a work presentation or before an important meeting, taking a few minutes to practice mindfulness can be an antidote to anxiety. Engaging in a brief mindfulness session means individuals can center themselves, lower their heart rate, and approach the task at hand with renewed focus and confidence.

Reflection and Journaling

Professionals can effectively teach their clients about the power of journaling and reflection following guided mindfulness sessions. Reflection after practicing mindfulness amplifies its benefits and encourages a deeper understanding of emotions and thought patterns. Journaling helps with the documentation of experiences and insights gained during mindfulness exercises. After each session, clients should be encouraged to write down their observations—any significant changes in mood, emerging thoughts, or shifts in physical sensations.

This reflective process helps recognize patterns and triggers, providing valuable insights into overall well-being and identifying areas that may need attention.

Sensory Grounding Meditations

Grounding techniques help bring awareness to the present moment by engaging the senses. Sensory grounding meditations use touch, sight, sound, smell, and taste to anchor attention, making them particularly useful for calming the nervous system, reducing anxiety, and cultivating mindfulness.

Script #3: Object Focus Meditation

1. Find a small object to hold—perhaps a smooth stone, textured piece of fabric, wooden bead, or crystal. Sit comfortably and close your eyes if you feel comfortable doing so.

2. (Pause for a few moments to settle.)

3. Take a deep breath in, and as you exhale, bring your awareness to the object in your hands. Feel its texture, its weight, its temperature. Notice every ridge, groove, or curve beneath your fingertips.

4. (Pause for 2-3 minutes to explore the object in silence.)

5. As thoughts arise, acknowledge them, then gently bring your focus back to the sensations in your hands. Explore the object as if you were discovering it for the first time. What do you notice?

6. If your mind drifts, return to the simple act of touching and holding. Let this object be a steady point of connection between you and the present moment.

7. (Pause for a few moments.)

8. When you're ready, take one final breath and slowly release the object, carrying this sense of presence with you.

Script #4: Color Spotting Meditation

1. Take a comfortable seat and begin by taking a deep, cleansing breath. Let your gaze soften as you slowly look around the space you're in.

2. Choose a color—perhaps blue, green, or red. Begin to scan your surroundings, looking for all the shades and variations of that color. Observe how it appears in different objects, noticing textures, shapes, and how light interacts with each one.

3. (Pause for 1-2 minutes, allowing time to explore the color in detail.)

4. Continue this for a few moments. If your thoughts begin to wander, simply return to your chosen color.

5. (Pause for a few moments.)

6. Now, shift to another color and repeat the process. As you explore the hues around you, feel yourself becoming more rooted in the present moment, more aware of the world as it is right now.

7. (Pause for 1-2 minutes.)

8. When you're ready, bring your attention back to your breath. Carry this sharpened sense of awareness with you as you continue your day.

Script #5: Scent and Memory Meditation

1. Select a scent that feels grounding—perhaps essential oil, fresh herbs, incense, or a familiar personal fragrance. Close your eyes and take a slow inhale, drawing the scent deeply into your awareness.

2. (Pause, allowing time to settle and observe the scent.)

3. Notice the first sensation it brings. Does it remind you of something? A place, a time, an emotion? Allow these impressions to come and go without clinging to them.

4. Instead, focus on the nuances of the scent itself. Is it sharp, soft, warm, or cool? Does it change as you continue breathing it in?

5. (Pause for 1-2 minutes.)

6. Let the fragrance anchor you fully in this moment. If your mind begins to wander, gently bring your attention back to the sensation of scent entering your body with each breath.

7. (Pause for 1-2 minutes.)

8. When you feel ready, take one final inhale, then slowly open your eyes. Carry this sense of calm and presence forward with you.

Instant Focus Meditations

The ability to maintain focus is a skill that directly affects our productivity and well-being. Meditation techniques provide significant support in this area by granting a structured way to develop clarity and concentration. Focus is more than just getting things done; it means improving overall performance and creating a sense of balance and well-being.

The Importance of Focus

Focus impacts productivity significantly, as it shapes how effectively we perform at work, in academics, or even in simple daily errands. When you can concentrate on one task without distraction, you're likely to complete it faster and with higher quality. This is because focused attention allows us to delve deeper into the task at hand, which increases our chances of finding innovative solutions and producing better outcomes. Studies have shown that people who regularly practice meditation tend to exhibit enhanced cognitive abilities, such as better memory retention and problem-solving skills, which are essential for productivity (Guerra, 2024).

Script #6: Guided Focus Script

A great way to help your clients achieve this kind of focus is through guided meditation, which brings a methodical approach to redirecting thoughts and setting intentions for clarity. To guide them in a guided focus meditation, share this script:

1. Guided meditation provides a structured way to redirect thoughts and set clear intentions. This short meditation will help cultivate focus and mental clarity. Let's begin.

2. Sit comfortably on a chair with your feet flat on the floor or the ground with your legs crossed. Close your eyes and take a deep breath in through your nose... then exhale slowly through your mouth. Repeat this a few times, allowing your body and mind to relax with each breath.

3. As you breathe out, imagine your thoughts settling like particles in a snow globe. Picture them swirling at first, then gently settling at the bottom, leaving a sense of calm and clarity in your mind.

4. (Pause for a few moments to let the image settle.)

5. Now, bring your full attention to your breath. Begin counting each inhale and exhale, slowly up to ten. Inhale—one, exhale—

two. Continue this pattern until you reach ten, then start again at one. If your mind wanders, gently bring your focus back to your breath without judgment.

6. (Pause for 2-3 minutes.)

7. Use this moment of clarity to set an intention for the day or the week ahead. Ask yourself: "What do I want to accomplish? How do I want to feel?" Envision yourself moving through these goals with ease, confidence, and focus.

8. Take one final deep breath in... and slowly exhale. Bring awareness back to your surroundings. When you're ready, gently open your eyes, carrying this sense of focus and clarity into your day.

Short and Effective

Meditations like the above highlight the rejuvenating effect that brief focus meditations can have for maintaining attention throughout the day. Even short bursts of meditation can refresh our mental state and allow us to return to tasks with renewed energy and perspective. The practice is not lengthy; even five minutes can make a difference in clearing mental clutter and improving concentration (Cervantes, 2024).

Encouraging Integration

Importantly, integrating focus meditations into various aspects of life can enhance group dynamics and individual sessions alike. Ending yoga classes or coaching sessions with a brief focus meditation can help participants assimilate their experiences and prepare to transition smoothly into the next part of their day. In group settings, starting or concluding meetings with a short meditation helps align the group's focus and creates a shared sense of purpose. For therapists and counselors, introducing clients to these techniques provides them with valuable tools they can use independently to manage stress and maintain focus outside of therapy sessions.

Short Gratitude Meditations

Gratitude can change the way we view and interact with the world, which reinforces a path toward emotional resilience and well-being. In understanding the psychological benefits of gratitude, we recognize it as more than just politeness or etiquette. Gratitude is an emotional response that significantly impacts mental health by reducing stress, enhancing mood, and increasing overall life satisfaction (Bournewood Staff, 2023). Studies have shown that engaging in gratitude practices regularly leads to lower levels of anxiety and depression, providing a buffer against life's challenges (Chowdhury, 2019).

Script #7: Guided Gratitude Meditation

Guided gratitude meditation sessions can be particularly effective in helping your clients gain this sense of appreciation and positivity. These sessions involve visualizations and affirmations that encourage people to focus on aspects of their lives for which they are grateful (Bournewood Staff, 2023). This script can be shared with clients:

1. Gratitude meditation helps cultivate appreciation and positivity by focusing on the people, experiences, and qualities that bring joy and meaning to life. This short guided meditation encourages visualization and affirmations to nurture a mindset of gratitude.

2. Sit or lie down in a relaxed position, allowing your hands to rest naturally. Close your eyes and take a deep breath in through your nose... and exhale slowly through your mouth. Let any tension in your body begin to soften.

3. Picture a peaceful scene—a place that brings you comfort and joy. It could be a quiet forest, a warm beach, or a cherished memory with loved ones. As you immerse yourself in this scene, allow a feeling of gratitude to grow within you. Notice the details—the colors, sounds, and sensations—letting them fill you with warmth and appreciation.

4. (Pause for 1-2 minutes to visualize and connect with the feeling of gratitude.)

5. Now, bring to mind three things you are grateful for today. They may be simple, like the warmth of the sun, a kind word from a friend, or the strength you've shown in difficult times. As you acknowledge each one, silently repeat an affirmation: "I am grateful for the goodness in my life." "I appreciate the love and support around me." "I welcome gratitude into my heart, letting it guide my day."

6. (Pause for 2-3 minutes to reflect.)

7. Take one final deep breath in... and exhale slowly. When you're ready, gently open your eyes, bringing this sense of gratitude with you into the rest of your day. Let it shape your perspective, filling even small moments with appreciation and joy.

Impact on Clients

This brief gratitude meditation not only reduces stress but also improves mood. Focusing on positive experiences and outcomes means clients can shift attention away from stressors and negativity, all while creating space for joy and contentment. This shift can lead to increased client engagement, as those who practice gratitude report feeling more connected and fulfilled (Chowdhury, 2019). Clients often find themselves more open to new experiences and interactions as well, leading to stronger relationships.

Practical Suggestions

Implementing gratitude meditations in various settings requires practical suggestions that cater to different environments and schedules. Here are some guidelines to consider:

1. **Integrating into Daily Routines**: Encourage clients to start or end their day with a short gratitude meditation. Whether at

home, in the office, or even during a commute, taking a few moments to reflect on what they are thankful for can make a significant difference.

2. **Creating a Dedicated Space**: Just as yoga involves setting a physical space for practice, establishing a designated spot for meditation—perhaps decorated with meaningful objects or symbols of gratitude—can enhance the meditative experience.

3. **Using Technology Mindfully**: There are numerous apps and online resources available that guide users through gratitude meditations. These tools can be particularly helpful for those new to the practice or looking to deepen their meditation experience.

4. **Adapting to Group Settings**: In group classes or therapy sessions, leading a collective gratitude mindfulness session can build community while reinforcing individual thankfulness. Sharing what each person is grateful for can enrich the practice, providing diverse perspectives and insights.

5. **Prompting Reflection**: Incorporate journaling prompts post-meditation to encourage reflection. Asking questions like "What am I most thankful for today?" or "How has gratitude changed my perspective?" can deepen awareness and solidify the benefits of the practice.

6. **Flexibility in Practice**: Recognize that individuals might connect differently with gratitude meditation. Offering variations, such as silent meditation, spoken affirmations, or visualization exercises, allows clients to discover what resonates best with them.

For professionals like yoga teachers, life coaches, therapists, and holistic practitioners, incorporating these gratitude techniques into your offerings provides clients with effective tools for managing stress and enhancing emotional health. Practitioners find that gratitude practices complement other wellness strategies and create a balanced approach to mental and emotional well-being.

Understanding Body Awareness

Body awareness is necessary for overall mental health, stress management, and emotional regulation. Consciously tuning into physical sensations means that those you work with can recognize areas of tension, gain acceptance, and develop a deeper connection with their body. Brief body scan exercises provide an effective way to cultivate this awareness while promoting relaxation.

Script #8: Guided Mini Body Scan Script

A mini body scan offers a structured yet brief method for releasing tension. You can guide clients through the following steps:

1. Find a comfortable position, either seated or lying down. Close your eyes gently and take a deep breath in, filling your lungs completely. As you exhale, allow your body to relax, releasing any tension you may be holding.

2. Bring your awareness to your feet. Feel them grounded, supporting you through every step of your life. Silently acknowledge their strength and endurance. With each breath, imagine warmth and appreciation flowing into them.

3. (Pause.)

4. Now, shift your attention to your legs. They carry you, move you, and support you. Offer them appreciation for their steadiness, their resilience. Breathe into them, releasing any tension that lingers.

5. (Pause.)

6. Move your focus to your torso—the center of your being. Feel your breath moving through your lungs, your heartbeat steady and strong. Acknowledge the quiet work your body does to

sustain you, moment by moment. Allow appreciation to settle here.

7. (Pause.)

8. Now, bring awareness to your arms and hands. These are the parts of you that create, embrace, and connect. Think of all they have done for you—holding, building, supporting, and expressing. Let appreciation fill them, releasing any tightness with each breath.

9. (Pause.)

10. Shift focus to your shoulders, neck, and jaw. These areas often carry stress. Imagine any tension melting away as you inhale deeply and exhale fully. Acknowledge the weight they carry and offer them kindness.

11. (Pause.)

12. Finally, bring your attention to your head—the space of thoughts, ideas, and awareness. Thank your mind for its ability to learn, process, and grow. Let any lingering tension dissolve as you take one last deep breath in... and a slow, peaceful exhale out.

13. (Pause.)

14. When you're ready, gently bring awareness back to the present. Move your fingers and toes, stretch if needed, and open your eyes. Carry this sense of appreciation with you throughout your day, knowing you are not just *doing* something—but *are* something deeply valuable.

Benefits of Body Scans

Mini body scans improve the body-mind connection and help clients recognize and respond to stress signals before they escalate. Regular practice improves emotional regulation, reduces anxiety, and creates a sense of inner calm, making it a valuable self-care tool.

Incorporating Into Practice

Wellness practitioners can integrate mini body scans into sessions as quick resets for clients that help them ground and refocus. These exercises are especially useful in high-stress settings, before meditation, or as a transition between activities. Personalizing the experience based on client needs enhances its impact.

Final Insights

In this chapter, we've explored how simple mindfulness techniques can be a game-changer for quick relaxation and stress relief. These scripts for brief meditation sessions are treasures for anyone needing to center themselves swiftly. These techniques help shift our attention from life's clutter to a place of calmness and balance.

Furthermore, integrating these mindfulness practices into everyday routines doesn't take much time but offers substantial benefits to those you work with. They are designed to fit seamlessly into busy schedules, whether during work breaks or quiet moments at home.

Chapter 3:

Moderate-Length Scripts for

Sustained Mindfulness

Guiding your clients through moderate-length meditation scripts can help them find a deep sense of awareness and presence in their daily lives. These thoughtfully crafted sessions are designed to provide a balance between accessibility and depth, which means that individuals at various stages of their mindfulness journey can immerse themselves without feeling overwhelmed.

In this chapter, we will work through several techniques that seamlessly integrate mindfulness into everyday activities. This chapter is filled with insights and strategies suitable for yoga teachers, life coaches, therapists, and holistic practitioners who seek to enhance their professional repertoire with enriched mindfulness practices. Each method discussed offers a unique way to deepen awareness, promote mental and emotional resilience, and ultimately support a balanced and mindful lifestyle in those with whom you work.

Fifteen-Minute Breathing Harmony

Breath can be a powerful tool for gaining inner peace and balance. Through using specific breathing techniques, those you work with can bring about a sense of relaxation and mindfulness that extends beyond the meditation session into daily life. Let's explore how these practices work and why they matter.

Breath Awareness Technique

Breath awareness involves paying attention to the natural rhythm of your breath without trying to alter it. This technique promotes relaxation by encouraging participants to observe the breath as it flows in and out through their nostrils, filling their lungs and leaving their body. These two extended meditation scripts are perfect for helping those you work with become comfortable with mindfulness and reap the benefits of a more extended mindfulness practice.

Script #9: Mindful Breath Awareness

This exercise leads to a deep sense of presence and relaxation by focusing on the natural rhythm of the breath. It helps calm the nervous system, increase mindfulness, and anchor attention to the present moment.

1. Begin by finding a comfortable position, either seated or lying down. Allow yourself to settle, releasing any tension in the body. If you're seated, rest your hands gently in your lap or on your thighs. If you're lying down, place your arms at your sides with palms facing up.

2. Gently close your eyes or soften your gaze. Take a moment to tune into your body, noticing any sensations or areas of tension. There's no need to judge—just observe.

3. Now, bring your awareness to your breath. Without changing it, simply notice how it flows in and out. Feel the coolness of the inhale, the warmth of the exhale. The breath is always here, always supporting you.

4. Let's take three deep breaths together. Inhale deeply through the nose... and exhale slowly through the mouth. Again, inhale... and exhale. One more time, filling the lungs completely... and releasing fully.

5. Now, allow your breath to return to its natural rhythm. Observe how it moves through you, rising and falling like waves on the shore.

6. With each inhale, imagine drawing in calm, clarity, and ease. With each exhale, release any tension, stress, or worry. There's no rush—just the gentle rhythm of your breath guiding you deeper into relaxation.

7. (Allow for 1-2 minutes of silence, with soft periodic reminders to return to the breath if needed.)

8. Now, begin to notice the pauses between breaths. The space at the top of the inhale... the stillness before the exhale... the moment of quiet before you breathe in again. Rest in these pauses, allowing yourself to fully experience the present moment.

9. If thoughts arise, simply acknowledge them and let them drift away, like clouds passing through the sky. There's no need to push them away—just return to the breath, again and again.

10. Now, expand your awareness. Feel your whole body breathing—your chest rising, your belly expanding, the gentle movement of air in and out. Imagine the breath flowing through every part of you, bringing fresh energy and renewal.

11. (Allow for 3-4 minutes of silence, guiding the listener back if needed.)

12. When you feel ready, begin to deepen the breath slightly. Inhale through the nose... exhale through the mouth.

13. Take a moment to notice how you feel. Carry this sense of calm and awareness with you as you slowly open your eyes, returning fully to the present moment.

Script #10: Breath and Color Awareness Practice

This practice combines breath awareness with color awareness to deepen relaxation and emotional balance. Each inhale draws in a healing color, while each exhale releases tension and negativity.

1. Find a comfortable position, either seated or lying down. Adjust your posture so that your body feels supported yet relaxed. Allow your hands to rest gently at your sides or in your lap.

2. Close your eyes or soften your gaze. Take a moment to arrive in this space, letting go of any distractions or thoughts about the day.

3. Bring your awareness to your breath, noticing how it moves in and out. No need to change it—just observe the natural rhythm.

4. Now, imagine a soft, glowing light above you. This light contains a color that represents healing, peace, or energy— whatever you need most in this moment. Let that color come to you naturally.

5. With your next inhale, picture this color entering your body, flowing through your nose, and spreading gently within. Feel it filling your chest, expanding into your arms, legs, and all the way to your fingertips and toes.

6. As you exhale, imagine a different color—one that represents tension, stress, or fatigue—leaving your body in a soft wave. See it dissolving into the air, carried away with each breath.

7. Continue this cycle: Inhale the nourishing color, exhale the releasing color. Each breath brings renewal. Each exhale brings release.

8. (Allow for 1-2 minutes of silence, guiding the listener back to the visualization if needed.)

9. Now, deepen this mental image. Picture the healing color gently wrapping around your heart center, expanding outward. With each breath, this color becomes more vibrant, filling your entire body with a sense of warmth and light.

10. If any areas of tension remain, direct the breath and color to those places. Imagine the healing color softening any tightness, dissolving any stress. Feel the tension melting away with each exhale.

11. (Allow for 3-4 minutes of silence, reminding the listener to stay with the visualization.)

12. Now, imagine the color growing beyond your body, surrounding you in a protective, comforting glow. It moves around you like a gentle aura, shielding you from negativity, holding you in a space of peace and balance. Rest here, breathing in this sense of wholeness and calm. Let your body, mind, and spirit be nourished by this energy.

13. (Allow for 3-4 more minutes of silence.)

14. When you are ready, begin to release the image. Allow the colors to fade, bringing your awareness back to the breath. Feel the gentle rise and fall of your chest, the natural rhythm of your breathing.

15. Slowly bring movement back to your fingers and toes. Stretch gently if it feels good. Take your time as you open your eyes, returning to the present moment.

16. Carry this sense of renewal with you as you move through the rest of your day.

This technique brings about a meditative state and promotes self-awareness. As participants continue to focus on their breath, they may notice thoughts entering their minds. When this happens, simply encourage your client to acknowledge them without judgment and allow them to drift away as they return their focus to breathing. This mindful approach enables participants to develop a peaceful detachment from unwanted thoughts to help them gain clarity and mental resilience (*Breath Meditation*, 2014).

Counting Breaths Practice

Another effective method is the counting breaths practice, which grounds the mind in the present moment through numerical focus. Many people find that counting each breath helps maintain focus and prevents the mind from wandering. It is also often used in Zen meditation—or *zazen*—and other mindfulness traditions.

Script #11: Counting Breaths Script

1. Welcome to this calming breathwork meditation, designed to anchor your mind and body through the practice of counting breaths. Find a quiet, comfortable position where you can sit or lie down with ease. Let your hands rest gently on your lap or by your sides, and allow your eyes to softly close.

2. Take a moment to notice your natural breath: the gentle rhythm of air moving in and out of your body. There's no need to change anything yet. Simply become aware.

3. Now, we'll begin a simple yet powerful practice: counting your breaths. The focus is not on matching inhales and exhales but on maintaining steady awareness of each breath by silently counting them.

    a. Inhale deeply through your nose, and mentally count "One."

    b. Exhale slowly through your mouth: "Two."

    c. Inhale again: "Three."

    d. Exhale: "Four."

    e. Inhale: "Five."

f.   Exhale: "Six."

g.   Breathe in: "Seven."

h.   Breathe out: "Eight."

i.   Inhale: "Nine."

j.   Exhale: "Ten."

4.   Once you reach ten, begin again at one, repeating the cycle for a several minutes. If your mind wanders, gently bring your focus back to the breath and start again at one. Let the counting be a soft anchor, keeping your awareness steady and present.

5.   (Pause for 5-6 minutes, allowing uninterrupted breath counting.)

6.   When you're ready, let go of the counting and simply observe your natural breath once more. Notice the calm that has settled within you: the gentle rhythm of your breath, the stillness of your mind.

7.   (Pause for a few moments to settle.)

8.   Slowly open your eyes, carrying this sense of centeredness with you into the rest of your day.

9.   Thank you for sharing this moment of breath and presence.

Starting with manageable goals, like a set period for meditation, and gradually increasing the time spent in practice can make sure that this exercise becomes a positive, sustainable habit—which is a piece of advice you can share with your clients. Regularly practicing at the same time each day helps embed mindfulness into your routine, allowing the benefits to flow more readily into your everyday life (*Breath Meditation*, 2014).

Movement Integration

Incorporating movement into a mindfulness practice can improve physical awareness. Movement Integration involves synchronizing simple movements with breath, further deepening the connection to both body and mind.

For those new to integrating movement, you can encourage them to start with simple exercises like lifting their shoulders on an inhale and releasing them on an exhale. This practice grounds them in the present and reinforces the connection between breath and bodily sensations. Over time, your clients may notice an improvement in overall coordination and a greater ease in performing daily tasks with mindful intention (*Breath Meditation*, 2014). Beyond that, these two extended meditation scripts can help you tie movement into your meditation practices shared with clients to improve mind-body wellness.

Script #12: Breath and Gentle Movement Synchronization

This practice deepens the mind-body connection by synchronizing breath with simple movements. It enhances physical awareness, grounds the body, and soothes the mind, making mindfulness more dynamic and engaging.

1. Find a comfortable position, either seated or standing. If seated, keep your spine tall but relaxed, with your hands resting on your lap or thighs. If standing, allow your feet to be hip-width apart, with a slight softness in your knees.

2. Close your eyes or lower your gaze. Begin by taking a few deep breaths, inhaling through the nose... and exhaling through the mouth. Feel the air moving in and out, settling into a natural rhythm.

3. Now, let's start integrating gentle movement. As you inhale, slowly lift your shoulders toward your ears. As you exhale, gently release them down, letting go of any tension. Repeat this for a few cycles, inhaling to lift, exhaling to soften.

4. (Guide through this movement for about 2 minutes.)

5. Now, shift your awareness to your arms. As you inhale, slowly raise your arms outward and upward, as if gathering energy. As you exhale, lower them back down, releasing any tightness. Move with ease, letting the breath guide the motion.

6. (Continue this movement for 2–3 minutes.)

7. Now, place your hands over your heart. With each inhale, imagine expanding your chest, filling your body with warmth. As you exhale, soften your shoulders, feeling a gentle release. Stay with this breath for a few moments, noticing any sensations.

8. (Pause for 1-2 minutes to deepen heart-centered awareness.)

9. Now, let's incorporate a gentle swaying movement. With each inhale, shift your body slightly to one side, and with each exhale, shift back to center. Then, on the next inhale, sway to the other side, exhaling back to center. Feel the rhythm, like a tree moving with the wind.

10. (Guide this for 2-3 minutes, allowing the listener to find their natural flow.)

11. Now, return to stillness. Observe how your body feels. Notice any warmth, tingling, or relaxation. Feel the breath moving through you, steady and calm.

12. (Pause for a few moments to absorb stillness.)

13. Slowly open your eyes, carrying this sense of awareness with you as you move through your day.

Script #13: Flowing Breath: A Continuous Movement Meditation

This practice focuses on smooth, flowing movements synchronized with breath to create a sense of calm and fluidity. It invites you to move like water—steady, gentle, and unbroken.

1. Find a comfortable standing or seated position. If standing, plant your feet firmly on the ground, hip-width apart. If seated, keep your spine long and hands resting lightly on your thighs. Soften your shoulders and close your eyes or lower your gaze.

2. Begin by taking a deep breath in through your nose... and exhale softly through your mouth. Let your breath become smooth and steady.

3. Let's start with a simple, flowing movement. As you inhale, sweep both arms out to the sides and up in a slow, graceful arc. As you exhale, lower them gently back down as if moving through water. Let the motion be continuous, each movement blending into the next without pause.

4. (Guide this for 2-3 minutes, encouraging smooth, rhythmic movement.)

5. Now, let's introduce a gentle skyward reach. As you inhale, lift your arms forward and up, reaching softly toward the sky. As you exhale, draw them back down with ease, keeping the flow unbroken. Imagine gathering calm energy on the way up and releasing tension as your arms lower.

6. (Guide this for 2-3 minutes, keeping the movement fluid.)

7. Finally, move into a soft opening and closing motion. Inhale as you extend your arms outward from the center of your chest, as if opening a large book. Exhale as you draw them back to the center, maintaining a smooth, effortless rhythm.

8. (Continue for 2-3 minutes, keeping breath and movement in harmony.)

9. Gradually slow the movements, letting your hands rest at your sides or on your lap. Take a few steady breaths, noticing the sensation of calmness and flow within your body.

10. When you're ready, gently open your eyes. Roll your shoulders back, take a final deep breath, and carry this sense of fluid grace with you throughout your day.

Awareness of Thoughts Meditation

Recognizing and observing one's thoughts without judgment is a vital skill when it comes to mindfulness. This practice improves self-awareness and leads to a deeper sense of peace and clarity in our minds. Let's delve into some techniques that can assist your clients in honing this ability.

Script #14: Thought Observation

This practice cultivates non-attachment to thoughts, helping individuals recognize them as passing mental events rather than absolute truths. Observing thoughts without identifying with them allows us to create space for greater clarity and emotional balance.

1. Find a comfortable position, either seated or lying down. If seated, sit with a tall but relaxed posture, hands resting gently on your lap. If lying down, allow your body to be fully supported, arms resting at your sides. Close your eyes or soften your gaze, bringing your attention inward.

2. Begin by taking a few deep breaths. Inhale deeply through your nose... and exhale slowly through your mouth. Again, inhale fully... and exhale completely. One more deep breath in... and let it go.

3. Now, allow your breath to settle into its natural rhythm, flowing effortlessly in and out. Bring your awareness to the present moment, simply noticing how your body feels.

4. Imagine yourself lying in an open field, gazing up at the sky. Thoughts may begin to arise—see them as clouds drifting overhead. Some are light and passing, others linger for a while. Let them come and go in their own time, without holding on or pushing them away.

5. (Allow for a pause, giving space for thoughts to arise.)

6. As a thought appears, acknowledge it without judgment. Silently label it: "thinking" or "a thought about..." and let it float on. There is no need to hold onto it, analyze it, or push it away. Simply watch it come and go.

7. (Guide this process for 2-3 minutes.)

8. If a strong thought arises—perhaps an anxious or repetitive one—recognize it for what it is: just a thought, not a truth, not a command. See it as a passing event in the mind, like a cloud drifting across the sky.

9. Return to your breath. Feel its steady rhythm anchoring you to the present. The breath is always here, even as thoughts continue to move.

10. (Allow another 2-3 minutes for silent observation.)

11. Now, gently bring your awareness back to your body. Notice any sensations, any feelings of lightness or clarity.

12. (Pause for a few moments.)

13. When you feel ready, softly open your eyes. Take a moment to notice how you feel—calm, present, unattached. Carry this sense of spaciousness with you as you move through your day.

Script #15: Labeling Thoughts Meditation

This practice cultivates awareness by mentally tagging thoughts as they arise. Through naming thoughts—such as "worry," "planning," or "judgment"—we gain an understanding of habitual thinking patterns, which in turn allows us to shift toward healthier mental habits with clarity and compassion.

1. Find a comfortable seated position, either on a chair with your feet planted on the ground or on a cushion with your legs crossed. Sit tall yet relaxed, allowing your shoulders to soften. Rest your hands gently on your lap or knees.

2. Close your eyes or lower your gaze. Take a deep breath in through your nose... and exhale slowly through your mouth. Again, inhale deeply... and exhale fully. Let your breath settle into its natural rhythm, steady and effortless.

3. Now, bring your awareness to the mind. Thoughts will naturally arise—this is part of the process. Rather than resisting them, we will simply observe and label them.

4. As a thought arises, pause for a moment. Gently name it without judgment. If it is about the future, you might label it as "planning." If it brings worry, simply name it "worry." If it's about analyzing something, call it "problem-solving."

5. There is no need to force labels or overthink them. Just gently name the thought and let it go, returning to the breath.

6. (Allow for 2-3 minutes of silence, guiding with occasional reminders to observe and label.)

7. If a strong or repetitive thought appears, notice it with curiosity. Does it fit into a pattern? Is it familiar? You may notice frequent labels like "self-judgment," "criticism," or "doubt." This is not about changing the thoughts—only recognizing them. With each inhale, bring in awareness. With each exhale, let go of attachment to the thought.

8. (Allow for another 2-3 minutes of silent practice.)

9. Now, gradually release the labeling process. Let go of the need to name each thought and simply return to your breath. Feel the spaciousness in your mind, the clarity in your awareness.

10. (Pause for 1-2 minutes of open awareness.)

11. Take a moment to observe how you feel. Has anything shifted? Do you notice any patterns? Carry this insight with you, using it as a tool for self-awareness in your daily life.

12. (Pause for reflection.)

13. Slowly open your eyes, returning to the present moment with renewed clarity.

Script #16: Breath as an Anchor

This practice helps cultivate mindfulness by using the breath as a steady focal point. The breath is always present, offering a way to anchor ourselves in the moment, especially when faced with overwhelming thoughts or emotions. Returning to the rhythm of breathing means we create stability, clarity, and a sense of calm.

1. Find a comfortable position, either seated with your back straight and hands resting on your lap or lying down with your arms at your sides. Close your eyes or soften your gaze, allowing yourself to settle into stillness.

2. Take a deep breath in through your nose... and exhale slowly through your mouth. Again, inhale deeply, filling your lungs... and exhale, releasing any tension. One more deep breath in... and let it go completely.

3. Now, allow your breath to return to a natural rhythm. Simply observe it without trying to control it. Notice the gentle rise and fall of your chest, the cool air entering your nostrils, and the warmth as you exhale.

4. The breath is your anchor, steady and unwavering. No matter where your mind wanders, the breath is always here, ready to guide you back to the present.

5. (Pause for a few moments, allowing space for awareness.)

6. As you continue to breathe, thoughts may arise. You might find yourself drifting to memories, to plans, or to worries. This is completely natural. When you notice this happening, gently acknowledge the thought, then return to your breath.

7. Each inhale is a fresh start. Each exhale is a release.

8. (Allow for 2-3 minutes of silent observation, occasionally reminding the listener to return to the breath.)

9. Now, bring a sense of curiosity to your breathing. Notice how the inhale expands your body… and how the exhale softens it. Feel the way your breath supports you, grounding you in this moment.

10. (Guide this awareness for another 2-3 minutes.)

11. If the mind becomes restless or distracted, simply refocus on the sensation of breathing. Imagine the breath as a steady anchor in shifting waters—no matter how strong the waves, you remain connected to this steady rhythm.

12. (Another brief pause to deepen the experience.)

13. Now, gently bring your awareness back to your surroundings. Notice any changes in how you feel. Has your mind settled? Do you feel more grounded?

14. When you're ready, softly open your eyes, carrying this sense of calm and stability with you into your day.

Script #17: Gentle Releasing

This practice leads to acceptance by allowing thoughts to drift away naturally, reducing mental clutter, and fostering inner peace. Instead of clinging to thoughts, we acknowledge them and release them with ease, creating a sense of freedom and lightness.

1. Find a comfortable position, seated or lying down. If seated, keep your spine straight but relaxed, with your hands resting on your lap. If lying down, allow your arms to rest naturally at your sides. Gently close your eyes or soften your gaze.

2. Take a deep breath in through your nose… and exhale slowly through your mouth. Again, inhale deeply… and exhale

completely, releasing tension with each breath. One more deep inhale... and let it go.

3. Now, allow your breath to flow naturally. Simply observe its rhythm without trying to control it. Feel the gentle rise and fall of your body with each inhale and exhale.

4. (Pause for 1-2 minutes, allowing space for awareness to settle before visualization.)

5. Imagine yourself standing beside a peaceful river. The water flows effortlessly, carrying leaves along its surface. These leaves represent your thoughts—some small and fleeting, others larger, drawing more of your attention.

6. As a thought arises, acknowledge it with kindness. There is no need to judge it or engage with it. Simply place it on a leaf and watch as the current carries it downstream. There is nothing to do—just observe and let go.

7. (Pause for a few breaths.)

8. Another thought may appear. Perhaps it is a worry, a memory, or an expectation. Recognize it, then gently place it on another leaf. Watch as it drifts away, carried by the water's steady movement.

9. (Allow for 2-3 minutes of silent practice, occasionally reminding the listener to let thoughts go.)

10. If a thought lingers, pulling you in, simply return to your breath. Feel its steady rhythm anchoring you in the present moment. With each exhale, imagine releasing any grasp on the thought, allowing it to float effortlessly away.

11. (Pause for 1-2 minutes again, letting the practice deepen.)

12. Now, shift your focus to the space between thoughts. Notice the stillness, the quiet. This space is always here, beneath the movement of the mind. Rest in this openness, allowing yourself to simply be.

13. (Guide this awareness for another 2-3 minutes.)

14. When you feel ready, bring your awareness back to your body. Notice any sensations of lightness, ease, or calm.

15. Take a deep breath in... and exhale fully. When you're ready, softly open your eyes, carrying this sense of release and serenity with you into the rest of your day.

For yoga teachers, life coaches, therapists, and holistic practitioners, incorporating these techniques into your professional repertoire can offer incredible benefits to those you guide. Educating students, clients, or patients about the value of non-judgmental thought observation can help them manage stress and improve mental clarity. It provides them with tools to navigate challenges with greater ease, leading to stronger mental health and emotional resilience.

Emotional Balancing Through Compassion

Cultivating self-compassion and extending kindness toward others is a powerful practice that promotes emotional regulation and stability. When we spend time changing our negative thoughts into positive affirmations, we initiate a healing process within ourselves. This is a wonderful concept to share with your clients.

This journey begins with the use of self-compassion phrases—simple but meaningful statements that challenge and overturn harsh self-criticism. When we consistently remind ourselves of our worth and embrace imperfections, we gain a helpful method for emotional healing. For example, instead of berating oneself for making a mistake, one can think, "I am human, I make mistakes, and that's okay."

Script #18: Self-Compassion Meditation

This practice nurtures self-kindness, acceptance, and understanding. Bringing awareness to our inner dialogue and embracing ourselves with the same warmth we would offer a dear friend means we develop a compassionate relationship with ourselves.

1. Find a comfortable position, either seated or lying down. Allow your hands to rest naturally—on your lap, at your sides, or gently placed over your heart if that feels comforting. Close your eyes or soften your gaze.

2. Take a deep breath in through your nose... and exhale slowly through your mouth. Again, inhale deeply, feeling your belly expand... and exhale, releasing any tension. One more deep breath in... and let it go completely.

3. Now, allow your breath to settle into a natural rhythm. With each inhale, invite in ease and warmth. With each exhale, release any tension or self-judgment you may be carrying.

4. (Pause for 1-2 minutes to allow presence to deepen before continuing.)

5. Bring your awareness inward. Notice how you are feeling in this moment—physically, emotionally, and mentally. There is no need to change anything, only to observe with gentle curiosity.

6. Now, imagine someone you love deeply—a close friend, a child, or even a pet. Picture how you would offer them kindness and support if they were struggling. Feel that warmth, that care, that unconditional love.

7. Now, gently turn that same compassion toward yourself. Imagine holding yourself in that same warmth, as if wrapping yourself in a soft, comforting embrace.

8. (Pause for a few breaths.)

9. Now, silently repeat these phrases to yourself, or modify them in any way that feels right for you:

    a. "May I be kind to myself."

b. "May I accept myself as I am in this moment."

c. "May I offer myself the same love I give to others."

d. "May I be patient with my struggles."

10. As you repeat these words, allow them to settle in, as though planting seeds of kindness within your heart. With each inhale, absorb their meaning. With each exhale, let go of self-criticism or doubt.

11. (Pause for 2-3 minutes, allowing the listener to internalize the phrases.)

12. If self-critical thoughts arise, acknowledge them gently. There is no need to push them away. Instead, imagine holding them with kindness, as you would a small child who is afraid or uncertain.

13. You might say to yourself: "I see this thought, but it does not define me." You are not your mistakes. You are not your flaws. You are human, deserving of the same kindness you offer others.

14. (Allow for another 2-3 minutes of quiet reflection, offering occasional reminders of self-kindness.)

15. Now, begin to deepen your breath. Feel the rise and fall of your body once more. Notice any shifts within you—perhaps a feeling of warmth, lightness, or ease.

16. (Pause for 1 minute to absorb and integrate these shifts.)

17. When you feel ready, slowly open your eyes, carrying this self-compassion with you.

As people become more at ease with themselves, the next step involves extending kindness to others. This act of kindness involves genuine empathy and understanding. When we approach others with this mindset, we develop stronger social relationships.

However, kindness isn't always easy to extend, especially toward challenging figures in our lives. But reframing negative emotions into compassion for such people can substantially lighten personal burdens. This approach helps us look past behaviors and to the underlying causes, which means we can also replace resentment or anger with compassion.

Script #19: Cultivating Kindness and Compassion for Others

This meditation focuses on extending kindness and understanding beyond ourselves. In developing genuine empathy, we strengthen our relationships and deepen our ability to connect with others. Even when kindness feels difficult, shifting our perspective can turn resentment into compassion.

1. Find a comfortable position, either seated or lying down. Allow your hands to rest gently on your lap, by your sides, or over your heart if that feels comforting. Close your eyes or soften your gaze.

2. Take a deep breath in through your nose... and exhale slowly through your mouth. Again, inhale deeply, feeling your belly expand... and exhale, releasing any tension. One more deep breath in... and let it go completely.

3. Now, let your breath settle into a natural rhythm, steady and effortless. With each inhale, invite in a sense of warmth and openness. With each exhale, release any heaviness or resistance.

4. (Pause for 1 minute to settle before visualizations.)

5. Begin by bringing to mind someone you care for deeply—someone who naturally inspires feelings of warmth and kindness within you. This could be a loved one, a close friend, or even a mentor who has supported you.

6. Picture this person clearly in your mind. See their face, the way they smile, the kindness in their eyes. Feel the connection you

share with them. As you breathe in, imagine filling your heart with warmth. As you breathe out, silently offer them these words:

    a. "May you be happy."

    b. "May you be healthy."

    c. "May you be safe and at peace."

7. Repeat these words slowly, allowing them to carry a sincere wish of well-being to this person.

8. (Pause for a few moments.)

9. Now, bring to mind someone neutral—perhaps a stranger you saw today, a colleague, or someone you pass in daily life but do not know well. Imagine their presence before you, recognizing that, just like you, they have joys and struggles.

10. Offer them the same words:

    a. "May you be happy."

    b. "May you be healthy."

    c. "May you be safe and at peace."

11. Let these words flow naturally from your heart, sending warmth and kindness outward.

12. (Pause for a few moments.)

13. Now, bring to mind someone you find challenging—someone who may have caused you frustration, hurt, or discomfort. Acknowledge any resistance that arises, but instead of pushing it away, hold space for it with gentle awareness.

14. Rather than focusing on their actions, try to see beyond them. Consider the possibility that they, too, carry struggles, fears, or

pain. With this awareness, extend compassion to them, repeating:

    a. "May you find peace."

    b. "May you be free from suffering."

    c. "May you experience kindness in your life."

15. You do not need to excuse their behavior, but you can choose to release resentment, replacing it with a sense of lightness and understanding.

16. (Pause for 2-3 minutes, allowing space for reflection.)

17. Now, expand this feeling outward. Imagine kindness radiating from your heart, reaching not just those you've focused on but extending beyond—to your community, your city, and the world as a whole.

18. See kindness flowing like ripples on water, touching every being with warmth and understanding. Know that each small act of compassion you offer creates a positive impact both within and around you. Rest in this feeling for a few moments, letting the warmth of kindness settle deeply within.

19. (Pause for 2-3 minutes, guiding them to stay with the sensation.)

20. Begin to bring awareness back to your breath, feeling the steady rise and fall.

21. Take one last deep inhale… and exhale fully.

22. When you feel ready, softly open your eyes, carrying this sense of kindness and understanding into the rest of your day.

Nature-Inspired Meditation

Reconnecting with nature through guided meditation is another great way to promote relaxation and inner peace. Engaging your senses and evoking the serene beauty of the natural world within your mind means you open up pathways for deeper awareness and peace. Descriptive imagery techniques are helpful with this process, as they allow you to create vivid mental pictures that draw you away from stress and into a space of calm.

Script #20: Descriptive Imagery Sanctuary

When practicing descriptive imagery, your clients can experience a deep state of peace and calm. Sharing this script can help them find sensory-based peace in the moment.

1. Find a comfortable position, either sitting or lying down. Allow your hands to rest gently at your sides or in your lap. Close your eyes if you feel comfortable doing so, or soften your gaze.

2. Take a slow, deep breath in through your nose... and exhale completely through your mouth. Let any tension begin to dissolve.

3. Again, breathe in deeply, feeling your belly rise... and exhale, releasing any lingering tightness. One more time—inhale, drawing in fresh energy... and exhale, letting go of stress. Now, allow your breath to settle into a natural, steady rhythm.

4. (Pause for 1-2 minutes to settle before entering imagery.)

5. With each breath, begin to imagine yourself in a place of deep peace—a sanctuary in nature where you feel completely at ease. This might be a lush forest, a tranquil beach, a sunlit meadow, or a quiet mountain trail.

6. Let your mind settle on a place that feels right for you. As you arrive in this space, take a moment to observe your surroundings. Notice the vibrant colors, the way the light filters through the trees, or reflects on the water. What do you see? Perhaps the golden hues of the sun setting over the ocean or the rich greens of tall trees stretching toward the sky.

7. (Pause for a moment.)

8. Now, shift your awareness to sound. Listen to the world around you—the rustling of leaves in the breeze, the rhythmic crash of waves, or the distant call of a bird. The sounds are soft, soothing, and natural, drawing you deeper into this peaceful moment.

9. (Pause.)

10. Next, notice the air on your skin. Is it warm with the gentle heat of the sun? Or cool and crisp like a morning breeze? Feel the air brushing against you, carrying with it a sense of freshness and renewal.

11. (Pause.)

12. Now, direct your focus to touch. Imagine the texture beneath you—the soft sand under your feet, the smooth rock you are sitting on, or the gentle sway of tall grass against your fingertips. Let yourself fully experience this sensation, grounding you in the moment.

13. (Pause.)

14. With each breath, you become more immersed in this peaceful sanctuary. You feel safe, supported, and deeply relaxed.

15. If your mind begins to wander, simply bring your awareness back to your surroundings. Notice the colors, the sounds, the sensations—let them draw you back into this moment of calm.

16. Now, take a few deep breaths, allowing this sense of peace to fill your entire being. With every inhale, you breathe in tranquility... with every exhale, you release tension.

17. (Pause for 2-3 minutes, allowing space for deep relaxation.)

18. Know that this place of peace is always within you. At any time, you can return here—simply by closing your eyes, connecting with your breath, and immersing yourself in the imagery.

19. Take a moment to set an intention: How would you like to carry this sense of calm into the rest of your day? Hold that intention gently in your mind.

20. (Pause for 1 minute to let the intention fully form and settle.)

21. Slowly, begin to bring your awareness back to the present moment. Notice your breath; steady and calm.

22. Take one final deep inhale... and exhale completely.

23. When you feel ready, softly open your eyes, carrying this sense of peace with you.

Script #21: Breathing With Nature

Integrating breath with nature further enhances mindfulness experiences. As your clients visualize natural scenes, help them align their breathing with the rhythms of the environment they imagine. Breath can keep them grounded while their mind explores these serene landscapes. This script is a great choice for helping your clients achieve this:

1. Find a comfortable position, either sitting or lying down. Let your hands rest gently in your lap or at your sides. Close your eyes if you would like, or soften your gaze.

2. Take a deep breath in... filling your lungs completely... and exhale slowly, releasing any tension.

3. Again, breathe in deeply... and exhale fully, letting your body settle into relaxation.

4. One more time—inhale... and exhale... allowing yourself to become fully present.

5. Now, let your breath find a natural, steady rhythm, flowing in and out like the gentle movement of nature itself.

6. (Pause for 1-2 minutes to deepen presence before beginning visualization.)

7. Begin to imagine yourself surrounded by nature—a place that brings you peace and tranquility. Perhaps you are standing in a vast meadow, walking along the shore of a quiet lake, or resting beneath the shade of an ancient tree.

8. Take a moment to let the scene form in your mind. Notice the colors, the textures, the way the light dances across the landscape.

9. (Pause.)

10. Now, listen. What do you hear? Maybe it's the rustling of leaves in the wind, the rhythmic waves against the shore, or the distant call of a bird. Let these sounds draw you deeper into the experience.

11. (Pause.)

12. As you immerse yourself in this peaceful environment, begin to sync your breath with its natural rhythm.

13. If you are near the ocean, imagine the waves rolling in with your inhale... and retreating with your exhale. Feel yourself breathing with the tide, a gentle and endless flow.

14. If you are in a forest, imagine the wind moving through the trees. With each inhale, the breeze gathers and rises... with each exhale, it drifts away, carrying tension with it.

15. If you are in a meadow, envision the grasses swaying. They rise as you breathe in… they settle as you breathe out. Your breath and nature, moving together in perfect harmony.

16. (Pause for a few moments.)

17. With each breath, feel your connection to the natural world deepen. The air you inhale is the same air that flows through the trees, across the mountains, and over the oceans.

18. As you exhale, imagine offering your breath back to nature, a continuous exchange of energy and life.

19. Breathe in peace, stability, and renewal… Breathe out tension, worry, and stress…

20. (Pause for 2-3 minutes, allowing for quiet reflection and breath synchronization.)

21. Now, as you continue to breathe, imagine nature responding to you. The earth beneath you supports you, holding you steady. The trees, the water, the sky—all embrace you with a quiet presence.

22. You are not separate from nature. You are part of its rhythm, its balance, its flow.

23. Let this realization fill you with a sense of grounding and peace. With each breath, you absorb this energy, carrying it within you.

24. (Pause for 1 minute to integrate the experience fully.)

25. Slowly, bring your awareness back to your body. Feel your breath, steady and calm. Notice the surface beneath you, the air around you.

26. When you feel ready, softly open your eyes, carrying the harmony of nature with you into the rest of your day.

The benefits of such practices extend beyond the immediate session. A post-meditation reflection can encourage your clients to explore the insights gained during these guided imagery sessions. Have them reflect on how the experience made them feel, what specific images or sensations stood out, and how they might influence their daily life.

Meditations can also incorporate elements that inspire positive emotions. Consider using a script where participants first imagine a sunrise. Ask them to see how the sky changes color, feel the warmth of the sun's rays, and notice how everything around them starts to glow. Such a scenario inspires hope and renewal—key components of sustained mindfulness. You can use this script to help:

Script #22: Sunrise of Renewal

1. Find a comfortable position, either sitting or lying down. Allow your hands to rest gently in your lap or by your sides. Close your eyes if you would like, or soften your gaze.

2. Take a deep, slow breath in… filling your lungs completely… and exhale gently, releasing any tension.

3. Again, inhale deeply… and exhale fully… letting your body relax.

4. One more time—breathe in calmness… and breathe out any remaining stress.

5. Now, allow your breath to find a natural, steady rhythm. Let it flow effortlessly, like a soft breeze moving through an open field.

6. (Pause for 1-2 minutes, allowing the breath to guide the listener into stillness.)

7. Picture yourself in a serene, open space—perhaps a quiet hilltop, a peaceful shoreline, or a wide meadow. The world around you is calm, resting in the final moments of night.

8. Above you, the sky is deep and dark, dotted with the last traces of starlight. The air is crisp and still, holding the quiet hush of early morning.

9. As you breathe in, feel the coolness of the night gently brushing against your skin. As you exhale, sense the subtle shift in the atmosphere, a quiet anticipation of the coming dawn.

10. (Pause.)

11. Now, turn your attention to the horizon. A soft glow begins to emerge, a delicate ribbon of gold stretching across the sky. The darkness starts to recede, making space for the first light of morning.

12. With each breath, watch as the sky changes... soft purples fade into vibrant pinks... deep blues dissolve into warm oranges. The world awakens slowly, moment by moment.

13. As the colors expand, feel a quiet warmth growing within you. This is the light of renewal, the gentle promise of a new beginning.

14. (Pause.)

15. Now, the sun's first golden rays break over the horizon, casting a soft glow on everything around you.

16. Feel the warmth of the sun on your skin. Imagine it touching your face, your hands, your heart. It is gentle, comforting, and full of life.

17. With each inhale, welcome this warmth into your body. Let it fill you with energy, with peace, with hope.

18. With each exhale, release any heaviness, any tension, any worries that no longer serve you.

19. Breathe in renewal... Breathe out anything you wish to let go of...

20. (Pause.)

21. As the sun rises higher, its light spreads across the landscape. The grass shimmers with morning dew, the water reflects golden hues, and the air hums with quiet life.

22. This light is within you, too. Feel it filling every part of your being, illuminating your heart, clearing your mind, renewing your spirit. You are bathed in warmth, in possibility, in peace.

23. Stay here for a few moments, simply breathing in this light... allowing it to refresh and restore you.

24. (Pause for 2-3 minutes, letting the participant immerse themselves in the sensation.)

25. Slowly, begin to bring awareness back to your body. Notice the rhythm of your breath, steady and calm. Feel the surface beneath you, the space around you.

26. Gently wiggle your fingers and toes, awakening movement in your body.

27. Take one final deep inhale... drawing in warmth, light, and renewal... and exhale fully, feeling refreshed and at peace.

28. When you're ready, softly open your eyes, carrying the energy of the sunrise with you into your day.

Remember, the effects of guided nature imagery accumulate over time. Encourage regular practice and periodic review of the outcomes to maximize benefits.

Concluding Thoughts

Together, we've explored how medium-length meditation scripts focusing on breathing can significantly enhance mindfulness and self-awareness. Through incorporating techniques such as breath awareness, counting breaths, and movement integration, practitioners can deepen their connection to the present moment. These practices nurture a state of inner calm and presence that extends beyond meditation sessions.

Beyond that, integrating such practices into professional settings gives students, clients, or patients the tools they need to manage stress more effectively and achieve greater emotional resilience. As you continue your journey with these methods, remember to encourage reflection and gratitude after each session in order to help solidify the benefits.

Chapter 4:

Extended Sessions for

Transformation and Growth

Extended sessions in meditation can be a great choice for incredible personal growth and healing. Engaging deeply with longer scripts can help your clients engage with self-awareness and reflection. These sessions encourage participants to explore their inner landscapes more thoroughly, providing fertile ground for lasting change and emotional growth. The extended format allows those participating to understand their subconscious better and more effectively. The process stimulates mental clarity and boosts emotional resilience, which can be invaluable in the modern world and with the stress that daily life brings.

In this chapter, we'll talk about how longer meditation scripts can guide you in helping your students and clients delve deeper into self-reflection. Furthermore, you'll learn what your clients need to incorporate regular self-reflection routines outside of guided sessions to maintain continuity in personal growth. Finally, we'll talk about overcoming challenges within self-reflection.

Deep Dive Into Self-Reflection

Introducing longer meditation scripts in extended sessions can be helpful when it comes to encouraging incredible personal growth and healing. To achieve this, you and your clients alike need to understand the intricacies of deep introspection and self-awareness. Understanding depth in self-reflection is a necessary factor for personal growth. It helps identify behaviors that require change and gain the insight needed to embark on a journey of continuous improvement.

Structured Prompts for Reflection

Structured prompts, such as guided questions and effective journaling techniques, can be great tools to share with your clients. They help with enhancing the self-discovery process. Through these prompts, you can inspire your clients to explore their thoughts and emotions more deeply. For example, asking "What patterns do I notice in my reactions to stress?" or "How do my values align with my current lifestyle?" can unlock insights that may have otherwise remained obscured. Journaling, when paired with these prompts, helps capture and analyze reflections, thus leading to a richer understanding of oneself. Some prompts that can be shared with clients for this purpose include:

- What emotions am I experiencing right now, and where do I feel them in my body?

- How do my values align with my current lifestyle, and where might I need to make adjustments?

- What limiting beliefs do I hold about myself, and how can I reframe them to support my growth?

- What are my short-term and long-term goals, and what small step can I take today to move closer to them?

- What am I grateful for in this moment, and how can I cultivate more gratitude in my daily life?

Creating a Reflective Space

The environment in which reflection takes place holds significant sway over its effectiveness. As a practitioner, establishing a serene and distraction-free space can help your clients engage in deep reflection by enhancing focus and introspection. A quiet room with calming music, gentle lighting, and comfortable seating helps create an atmosphere conducive to exploring the depths of one's mind, especially during extended meditation sessions. This intentional setting minimizes external disturbances so that clients can concentrate wholly on the internal experience.

Integration of Insights

Integrating insights from reflective practices benefits the growth of your clients.

You should encourage your clients to maintain regular self-reflection routines beyond guided sessions. In doing so, they can consistently engage with their evolving thoughts and emotions and make reflection a habitual part of their lives. Regular practice helps solidify the connection between self-awareness and growth. Over time, your clients will become more adept at identifying and addressing areas in need of change, which creates a proactive approach to personal development.

Guided Visualization Journey

Guided visualizations have immense power when it comes to healing and goal manifestation. This practice leverages the power of imagination to dissolve mental barriers, reduce anxiety, and create a sense of safety and creativity for clients.

The benefit of guided visualization is its ability to engage the imagination intensely. It works with the brain's natural tendency to respond to imagined scenarios almost as vividly as it does to real experiences. Through carefully constructed images and experiences, you can help your clients visualize desired outcomes or embrace serene environments, which also generate feelings of peace and confidence.

Crafting Effective Visualizations

Creating effective guided visualizations benefits from personalization. Using tailored imagery and descriptive language that suits each client you work with can help resonate with their unique needs and aspirations. When visualizations are crafted with the individual in mind, they become more relatable and impactful. This personalization boosts client engagement and enriches the overall experience, allowing individuals to immerse themselves fully in the visualization journey.

Visualization Techniques

Various visualization techniques are available to achieve specific outcomes. Nature imagery, for example, can encourage relaxation by immersing clients in tranquil scenes like a peaceful forest or a gentle ocean tide. Future-self visualizations, on the other hand, encourage participants to imagine their lives after achieving their goals, motivating them to work towards these futures. These techniques relax the mind and inspire action by helping clients visualize the steps required to reach their desired destinations. Such approaches have been shown to lower anxiety levels and improve overall well-being (West, 2022).

Measuring Impact

Another important aspect of using guided visualizations in your practice is measuring their impact. To ensure that sessions are beneficial, you can help your clients track their responses over time. This involves listening to feedback and adjusting visualizations to better suit changing needs. Techniques such as regular check-ins and follow-up discussions can gauge how clients are progressing and identify areas that may require adjustments. Furthermore, encouraging journaling as part of the process offers clients an opportunity to reflect on their experiences, insights, and emotions.

Script #23: Pathway to Growth

This script can help you encourage your clients to use guided visualization for strengthened growth. You can modify this script as needed to suit the needs of the individuals you work with, or you can use it as is.

1. Find a position where you can be both relaxed and alert. If sitting, keep your back straight but not rigid. If lying down, allow your body to settle naturally.

2. Take a slow, deep breath in through your nose... and exhale through your mouth. Again—inhale, steady and controlled... exhale, releasing any unnecessary tension.

3. With each breath, let your shoulders drop. Loosen your jaw. Let your hands rest comfortably. Nothing forced, just letting go of anything you don't need to hold onto right now.

4. Now, shift your focus to the natural rhythm of your breath. You're not trying to change it—just noticing. With every inhale, you bring in focus. With every exhale, you clear space for what matters.

5. (Pause 30 seconds.)

6. Imagine yourself standing at the start of a path. The way ahead is clear, well-lit, and steady. This path represents progress— your ability to move forward with intention.

7. (Pause for a few moments.)

8. Take a step. Feel the ground beneath you—solid, dependable. With each step, you set something down. First, excess worry— acknowledge it, then leave it behind. Next, self-doubt— recognize it, then let it go. Then, the weight of past mistakes— take the lesson, but don't carry the burden.

9. Step by step, you move forward with more clarity, feeling lighter, more focused, more capable.

10. (Pause 1 minute.)

11. Ahead, you see a threshold—a simple, open doorway. It marks a shift from where you've been to where you're going. Step up to it. Pause for a moment. You don't need permission to step through—it's your choice.

12. (Take a breath. Then step forward.)

13. Feel the difference. A subtle but real shift. You're standing in a space where you define the next move.

14. (Pause 1 minute.)

15. In front of you, there is a reflective surface—a pool of water, still and steady. You walk up to it and look at your own reflection.

16. You see yourself not as you were but as you are at your best. Capable. Clear-minded. Unshaken by the past.

17. This version of you isn't something to chase—it's already there. It always has been.

18. Reach down and touch the water. Watch the ripple expand outward, reinforcing this shift. Let this image settle in.

19. (Pause for 2 minutes.)

20. Now, take one last deep breath, locking this feeling in.

21. Turn back toward the path. You are still you—but clearer, more intentional, more grounded. The path continues, and you carry this mindset forward.

22. When you're ready, bring awareness back to your body. Feel the surface beneath you. Notice your breath.

23. Wiggle your fingers, your toes. Take one more breath in... and as you exhale, open your eyes.

24. Welcome back.

Script #24: Ocean of Possibilities

This script also uses the power of visualization, instead focusing on possibility—something that can be deeply inspiring for improvement.

1. Find a comfortable position, allowing your body to relax fully. Close your eyes and take a deep breath in... feeling your abdomen expand... and exhale slowly, releasing tension. Breathe in again, drawing in fresh energy... and breathe out, letting go of anything unnecessary.

2. With each breath, allow your body to settle. Notice the steady rhythm of your heartbeat. Let your breath flow naturally, like waves rolling onto the shore.

3. (Pause for 1 minute.)

4. Now, visualize yourself standing on a quiet beach. The sand beneath your feet is firm and supportive. Ahead, the horizon stretches endlessly where the sky meets the ocean.

5. Above, the early light of day emerges, casting a soft glow across the water. A gentle breeze moves past, cool and refreshing. The steady rhythm of the waves creates a sense of ease, inviting you to relax more deeply.

6. Take a step forward, feeling the ground shift slightly beneath you. The ocean represents something greater—your potential, your resilience, and your ability to move forward. Walk toward the water, letting the tide touch your feet.

7. (Pause for 2 minutes.)

8. With each wave, allow something unnecessary to be carried away.

9. Inhale deeply... and as you exhale, let go of tension.

10. Inhale again… and as you exhale, release self-doubt.

11. One more breath in… and as you exhale, create space for clarity and perspective.

12. With every breath, feel yourself becoming more present.

13. (Pause 1 minute.)

14. Now, step further into the water. The temperature is steady—cool, refreshing, yet comfortable. As you move deeper, the water lifts you, allowing you to float effortlessly.

15. The ocean supports you, holding you in a space of stillness. Above, the sky expands infinitely. Below, the water flows freely, clearing away anything that no longer serves you.

16. Remain in this space for a moment, letting your body and mind settle.

17. (Pause 2 minutes.)

18. As you float, a quiet sense of clarity emerges—a feeling of balance, of knowing, of perspective.

19. If any thoughts, insights, or realizations arise, simply observe them. If not, simply remain here, present in this moment.

20. (Pause 2 minutes.)

21. Gradually, begin to drift back toward the shore, carrying with you this sense of clarity.

22. As you step onto the sand, take a final look at the ocean. Know that this space is always within reach—available whenever you need stillness, perspective, or a moment to reset.

23. Take a deep breath, allowing this sense of clarity to settle into your body.

24. Bring awareness back to the present. Feel the surface beneath you. Notice the rhythm of your breath.

25. When you're ready, open your eyes.

26. Carry this awareness forward.

Heart Opening Meditation

In a world where personal relationships and inner peace are often strained, heart-centered practices can help reconnect us through compassion and love. These practices emphasize expanding heart energy, which is necessary for empathy and enhancing our relationships with others.

Understanding heart-centered practices requires the acknowledgment of their profound impact on personal and interpersonal growth. These practices aim to open the heart to both giving and receiving love. This openness helps dissolve barriers that prevent genuine connection, thereby leading to the development of empathy. Empathy, as we know, is central to healthy relationships, allowing us to see the world from another's perspective and respond with kindness and understanding. Expanding heart energy encourages this empathetic interaction and improves how we relate to others and deepen connections with those around us.

Techniques for Heart Opening

An effective way to facilitate heart-opening experiences is through techniques like breathwork, affirmations, and movement. Breathwork enhances emotional clarity and promotes relaxation, which in turn makes it easier to access feelings of love and compassion. Affirmations, particularly those focused on self-love and acceptance, reinforce positive thought patterns. Phrases like "I am worthy of love" or "I embrace my true self" can be integrated into daily routines to shift internal dialogue and create a loving outlook (Conway, 2025).

Movement, especially through yoga and dance, is another method for heart-opening experiences. Engaging the body allows clients to release pent-up emotions and express themselves freely.

Script #25: Expanding Love and Compassion

This meditation script is perfect for encouraging your clients to open their hearts and reap the benefits of doing so.

1. Find a comfortable seated or lying-down position. Allow your hands to rest gently over your heart, feeling the warmth of your touch. Close your eyes softly, signaling to your mind that it's time to turn inward.

2. Take a deep inhale through your nose... and exhale fully through your mouth, releasing tension. Again, inhale... and exhale, sinking deeper into relaxation. With each breath, feel yourself becoming more present, more open.

3. Notice your heartbeat. The steady rhythm, the quiet strength. It has been with you since the beginning, always guiding, always giving. As you breathe, imagine your heart as a flower—gently closed, yet full of potential. With each inhale, it begins to bloom, opening petal by petal.

4. (Pause for 1 minute, let this image of blooming settle and take shape.)

5. Now, bring awareness to your breath. We will practice heart-focused breathing, a technique that synchronizes your breath with the energy of love and compassion. Breathe in deeply through your nose for a count of four... hold for four... and exhale slowly for six. Again, inhale for four... hold for four... exhale for six.

6. With each breath, imagine golden light flowing into your heart, filling it with warmth and openness. On your inhale, breathe in love. On your exhale, release any tension or heaviness.

7. Inhale... expanding your heart space. Exhale... letting go of anything that closes you off from love. Continue for a few more breaths, feeling your heart grow lighter and more radiant.

8. (Pause 1 minute.)

9. Now, silently or aloud, repeat these affirmations, letting their truth resonate within you. As you say these affirmations, feel them sinking into your heart space, rewriting any old beliefs that have kept love at a distance. With each breath, these words become a part of you:

    a. "I am open to love and connection."

    b. "I give and receive love freely."

    c. "I am worthy of deep, unconditional love."

    d. "My heart is expansive, filled with kindness and understanding."

    e. "I release fear and embrace love."

10. Now, if you are seated, place your hands on your knees. If you are lying down, let your arms rest by your sides. We will use gentle movements to further open the heart.

11. On your inhale, gently roll your shoulders back, lifting your chest slightly. On your exhale, allow your shoulders to soften, releasing any tightness. Repeat this movement, linking it with your breath, feeling your heart space expanding.

12. Now, if comfortable, place your hands behind you, fingertips resting on the ground or seat behind you. Gently lift your chest toward the sky, opening through the front of your body. Hold this for a few breaths, letting your heart energy radiate outward.

13. If lying down, imagine your chest opening effortlessly, as if sunlight is pouring into your heart space, warming and softening it.

14. (Pause 1 minute.)

15. Now, imagine a warm, golden light glowing at the center of your chest. This is your heart's energy, your source of love and connection. With each inhale, this light grows stronger... expanding outward. It fills your entire chest, radiating into your arms, your hands, your whole body.

16. Now, visualize this light extending beyond you—like rays of the sun, touching the people you love. See it reaching out to family, friends, even strangers. As this light expands, feel a deep sense of connection. A knowing that love is always within you, always available to give and receive. Sit in this radiant energy, letting your heart be fully open.

17. (Pause 1 minute, let the warmth and expansion settle deeply.)

18. Slowly bring awareness back to your physical body. Feel your hands resting where they are. Notice the softness in your heart space, the warmth within. Take a deep inhale... and exhale with a sigh.

19. Before you open your eyes, reflect: How does your heart feel at this moment? What are you taking with you from this practice?

20. Hold this feeling of openness and love as you gently return to the present. When you're ready, softly blink your eyes open, carrying this heart-centered energy into your day. Your heart is open. You are love. You are loved.

Manifestation and Abundance Meditation

Manifestation practices promise opportunities for incredible growth when practiced correctly for personal development and healing. If those you work with have a potential interest in using manifestation to meditate on their goals and needs, then this can be a game-changer for your practice.

To start, let's dive into the basis of manifestation. It's not just wishful thinking. Manifestation means actively aligning your psychological state with your aspirations. Doing so also means developing a mindset where your emotions and thoughts resonate with your goals. The energy behind every thought and emotion has a big impact on our experiences. Positive, intentional thoughts coupled with aligned emotions can indeed set the stage for favorable outcomes (Groh, 2024).

Guided Script for Manifestation

You can help your clients with this process through guided scripts that utilize visualizations and affirmations. When clients vividly imagine their goals, it helps bridge the gap between their current state and their desired reality. Likewise, affirmations are positive statements repeated to reinforce belief and motivation. Using affirmations daily improves gratitude and keeps the focus sharp on one's goals. This script is carefully crafted to help your clients work with manifestation to reach their goals.

Script #26: Aligning With Your Desires

1. Find a quiet, comfortable space where you can be undisturbed. Sit or lie down in a way that allows your body to relax completely. Gently close your eyes, signaling to your mind that it's time to turn inward.

2. Take a slow, deep inhale through your nose… and exhale fully through your mouth. Again, inhale… and exhale, releasing tension. With each breath, feel your body becoming lighter, more open.

3. Now, bring your awareness to the present moment. Let go of any lingering thoughts about the past or future. This moment, right here, is where your power exists. This is where manifestation begins.

4. (Pause 1 minute, allow stillness to settle in.)

5. Now, bring to mind a goal, desire, or aspiration. It could be related to love, success, health, or creativity—whatever feels most aligned with you at this moment. Hold this vision clearly in your mind's eye. See yourself already living this reality. What does it look like? What do you see around you?

6. Now, step deeper into the visualization. What do you hear in this reality? Are there sounds of celebration, laughter, or joy? What do you feel? Is there a sense of peace, excitement, or gratitude? Immerse yourself completely in this vision, allowing your heart to expand with belief. This reality is already on its way to you.

7. (Pause 1 minute, let the vision grow vivid.)

8. Now, let these affirmations settle into your being, shifting your energy to one of deep trust and receptivity:

    a. "I am aligned with abundance."

    b. "Everything I desire is flowing toward me."

    c. "I trust in the unfolding of my dreams."

    d. "I am worthy of receiving all that I seek."

9. Place both hands over your heart. Feel the steady, rhythmic beating. This is the pulse of life, always moving forward, always creating.

10. Breathe deeply into your heart space. Now, imagine your heart as a golden vessel, open and ready to receive the blessings the universe has in store. With every inhale, this vessel fills with radiant energy—opportunities, love, prosperity, and joy. With every exhale, you release any lingering resistance, allowing yourself to receive fully.

11. Repeat silently or aloud:

    a. "I am open to receiving abundance."

     b. "Blessings flow effortlessly into my life."

     c. "My heart overflows with gratitude."

12. Feel yourself expanding, making room for all that is coming.

13. (Pause for 1 minute.)

14. Gratitude is the frequency of abundance. The more you express gratitude, the more the universe responds in kind. Think of three things you are deeply grateful for—things that already exist in your life. Let that gratitude fill your heart, amplifying your energy of abundance.

15. Now, think of three things you desire… but express gratitude as if they have already arrived. Gratitude turns desires into reality. Let yourself bask in this energy of appreciation.

16. (Pause 1 minute.)

17. Slowly bring awareness back to your physical body. Feel the support beneath you, the air around you, the life within you. Take a deep inhale… and exhale with a soft sigh.

18. Before opening your eyes, hold one last moment of intention. Say to yourself:

     a. "My desires are already manifesting."

     b. "I am a magnet for success, love, and joy."

     c. "I trust in divine timing and alignment."

19. When you're ready, gently blink your eyes open, carrying this energy of manifestation with you. Your vision is already in motion. Believe, receive, and create.

Creating an Abundance Mindset

Transitioning to an abundance mindset is another aspect of effective manifestation that you can share with your clients. This involves breaking free from limiting beliefs—those insidious thoughts that suggest unworthiness or impossibility. Guiding your clients to challenge these beliefs actively means that you can help them reframe their unhealthy thinking patterns. Celebrate small victories along the way to reinforce progress and build confidence. Beyond that, incorporating gratitude practices into daily routines enhances this transformation.

Evaluating Manifestation Success

An integral part of practicing manifestation involves evaluating its success effectively. Setting checkpoints can be a great way to help your clients monitor their progress and maintain momentum. Sharing stories with peers or in group sessions can also improve accountability and provide motivational boosts through collective support. Story-sharing not only solidifies individual achievements but also inspires others to persevere. Finally, reinforcing accountability ensures that clients remain committed to their personal growth by promoting continuous action toward their goals.

Empowerment Through Self-Acceptance

Self-acceptance is the basis of personal empowerment and growth. It helps people embrace both their strengths and imperfections without judgment, develop resilience and confidence, and gain a sense of inner peace. Many people struggle with self-criticism and unrealistic expectations, which can create barriers to growth and emotional well-being. Through cultivating self-acceptance, we create space for healing, self-compassion, and authentic living.

Guiding your clients through this process is worthwhile. Self-acceptance-based meditations and exercises can help them break free from self-imposed limitations and develop a healthier relationship with themselves. Many different techniques exist to help with cultivating self-acceptance, all of which can be incorporated into meditation sessions as you see fit. Some of those techniques include:

- Mindfulness and Awareness: Encouraging clients to observe their thoughts and emotions without judgment.

- Affirmations: Repeating positive statements that reinforce self-worth, such as "I accept myself fully as I am."

- Self-Compassion Exercises: Practicing kindness toward oneself, especially in moments of perceived failure.

- Visualization: Imagining a future self who has fully embraced personal worth and confidence.

- Journaling: Reflecting on progress, emotions, and patterns of self-talk.

Meditation is a particularly effective tool for developing self-acceptance, as it allows clients to cultivate inner awareness and reframe limiting beliefs. The following script can be shared with clients to help them connect with and embrace their authentic selves.

Script #27: Embracing Self-Acceptance

1. Find a comfortable seated or lying-down position. Close your eyes and take a deep, cleansing breath in through the nose… and exhale slowly through the mouth. With each breath, allow your body to soften. Inhale deeply, filling your lungs… and exhale, releasing any tension. With every breath, imagine yourself sinking deeper into relaxation.

2. (Pause for 30 seconds.)

3. Gently bring your awareness to your body. Notice how it feels without judgment. Perhaps there is tension, restlessness, or stillness. Whatever you feel, acknowledge it with kindness.

4. (Pause for 30 seconds, letting participants observe their physical state.)

5. Now, shift your attention to your thoughts. Observe them as if they are clouds passing in the sky—without attaching to them, without resistance. Take another deep breath in... and exhale fully.

6. (Pause for 30 seconds.)

7. Repeat silently to yourself:

   a. "I allow myself to be as I am."

   b. "I accept this moment fully."

   c. "I release self-judgment."

8. (Pause for 30 seconds.)

9. Place a hand over your heart, feeling its steady rhythm. This heart has been with you through every challenge, every success, every moment of your life.

10. (Pause for 30 seconds, allowing time to connect with the heartbeat.)

11. Now, bring to mind a time when you were hard on yourself. Maybe you felt like you weren't good enough or that you had to prove your worth. Without judgment, acknowledge that moment. Allow yourself to see it with compassion.

12. (Pause for 45 seconds, give gentle room for emotional reflection.)

13. Now, imagine yourself as a child—pure, innocent, deserving of love. Speak to that younger version of yourself with kindness.

14. Repeat silently:

    a. "I am enough, exactly as I am."

    b. "I embrace my strengths and imperfections."

    c. "I am worthy of love and acceptance."

15. Let these words settle deep into your heart.

16. (Pause for 1 minute.)

17. Now, bring your awareness to the center of your chest, where a sense of warmth begins to form. This warmth represents unconditional self-acceptance. With each inhale, feel it spread through your body, growing deeper and more comforting. With each exhale, release any remaining doubt or self-criticism.

18. (Pause for 1 minute.)

19. Feel this warmth filling every part of you—your mind, your heart, your soul. You are whole. You are worthy. You are enough. Breathe in this truth... and exhale any resistance.

20. Repeat silently:

    a. "I trust myself."

    b. "I honor my journey."

    c. "I fully embrace who I am."

21. (Pause for 1 minute.)

22. Slowly bring awareness back to your breath, to your body resting in this space. Feel the ground beneath you, supporting you completely.

23. (Pause for 30 seconds.)

24. Take one final deep breath in... and as you exhale, gently open your eyes. Carry this energy of self-acceptance with you, knowing that you are always enough, exactly as you are.

Summary and Reflections

In this chapter, we took a look at longer meditation scripts for deep personal transformation and healing. Using guided questions and journaling can help your clients explore thoughts and emotions with newfound depth. Beyond that, encouraging regular self-reflection beyond structured sessions empowers your clients to make self-awareness a consistent part of their journey, which leads to continual improvement.

We also looked closely at guided visualizations and heart-opening meditations as tools for enhancing mindfulness and emotional well-being. These practices encourage people to visualize desired outcomes, tap into their imagination, and connect more deeply with themselves and others. Tailoring these techniques to each client's unique needs makes them even more impactful.

Chapter 5:

Incorporating Breathwork Into

Practice

Incorporating breathwork into your practice can enhance meditation sessions by unlocking a whole new level of calmness and focus for participants. Simply tuning into the rhythm of their breath helps them develop a deeper connection with themselves, both mentally and physically. Whether you're guiding someone through yoga, coaching a client, or supporting someone in therapy, breathwork is a great method for mindfulness that is both accessible and highly effective. This chapter explores this relationship, showing how various breath techniques can turn a regular meditation session into a more mindful experience.

Breathwork for Anxiety

Breathwork is an effective tool for managing anxiety, a common experience that can disrupt daily life and well-being. Breathwork has the ability to activate the parasympathetic nervous system, which leads to relaxation and brings a sense of calm to the mind and body (Department of Health & Human Services, 2015).

A helpful aspect of using breathwork for anxiety management is its focus on enhancing self-awareness. As your participants tune into your breathing patterns, they can better understand how their body responds to stress. This awareness allows them to catch signs of anxiety early and employ breathing techniques to prevent escalation.

Scripts for Meditating and Reducing Anxiety

Let's explore some specific breathing scripts designed to reduce anxiety. These scripts are useful tools that clients can incorporate into their routines.

Script #28: The Physiological Sigh

This meditation focuses on using the physiological sigh to quickly regulate the nervous system, reduce stress, and restore balance. The physiological sigh consists of a double inhale followed by a slow, controlled exhale.

1. Find a comfortable position, either seated or lying down. Gently close your eyes if that feels comfortable.

2. Take a moment to check in with your body. Notice any areas of tension or any tightness in the chest, shoulders, or jaw.

3. Now, begin by taking a slow, deep breath in through your nose... and exhale naturally through your mouth.

4. Again, inhale deeply... and exhale slowly. Let yourself settle into the rhythm of your breath.

5. (Pause for 30 seconds.)

6. Begin the physiological sigh. This breath pattern consists of two inhales followed by an extended exhale. The first inhale fills the lungs, while the second, shorter inhale maximizes oxygen intake. The long exhale releases carbon dioxide, signaling your nervous system to shift into a more relaxed state.

7. Take a deep breath in through your nose... now sip in a little more air at the top of your inhale...

   a. Hold for a brief moment...

b. Now, exhale fully and slowly through your mouth, allowing your body to soften.

c. Repeat: Inhale—small inhale—exhale.

8. Now, continue this at your own pace. Double inhale through the nose… and a long, controlled exhale through the mouth.

9. (Pause for 3 minutes, guiding the breath if needed.)

10. Now, allow your breath to return to a natural rhythm. Notice how your body feels. Perhaps there's a sense of relief, steadiness, or ease.

11. As you breathe normally, remind yourself that this technique is always available to you. You can use it whenever you feel anxious, overwhelmed, or simply need to reset.

12. Take one more deep breath in… and exhale slowly.

13. Gently bring awareness back to your surroundings. Wiggle your fingers and toes, and when you're ready, open your eyes.

Script #29: 1:2 Breathing

This meditation guides your participants through a 1:2 breathing technique, which is a simple but effective way to reduce stress and promote calm. Lengthening the exhale as this method requires activates the body's relaxation response and helps bring a sense of balance and clarity.

1. Begin by finding a comfortable position. Sit with your back straight but relaxed, or lie down if that feels more comfortable. Close your eyes or soften your gaze.

2. Take a moment to observe your breath as it is. No need to change anything—simply notice the rhythm of your inhale and exhale.

3. Now, take a slow, deep breath in through your nose... and exhale gently through your mouth. Let yourself settle into this space of stillness.

4. (Pause for 30 seconds.)

5. We will now begin the 1:2 breathing exercise. In this technique, we will inhale for 4 counts and exhale for 8 counts, proportional to a 1:2 ratio. The exhale will be longer than the inhale, allowing your body to release tension and invite calm.

   a. Inhale... 1... 2... 3... 4...

   b. Exhale... 1... 2... 3... 4... 5... 6... 7... 8....

   c. Inhale... 1... 2... 3... 4...

   d. Exhale... 1... 2... 3... 4... 5... 6... 7... 8....

6. Continue this pattern on your own, focusing on the rhythm of your breath. Inhaling just for a moment, and then exhaling fully to release any tension or stress. If your mind wanders, gently guide it back to the breath.

7. (Pause for 3 minutes, guiding if necessary.)

8. Gently release the breath pattern and return to your natural breathing. Notice how your body and mind feel. Perhaps you feel more relaxed, more present, or more grounded. Take a moment to acknowledge the power of your breath as a tool you can use anytime you need to regain focus and calm.

9. Take one final deep breath in... and exhale fully. When you're ready, bring movement back to your body and open your eyes.

These breathwork practices align seamlessly with various professional settings, such as yoga studios, therapy offices, and life coaching sessions.

The versatility of breathwork means it integrates effortlessly into holistic approaches to wellness. For practitioners, breathwork creates a connection between physical, mental, and emotional health, which encourages balance at all levels. It complements other mindfulness methods as well.

Balancing Breath Techniques

Breathwork is an incredible tool for achieving balance in physical, emotional, and energetic states. With these scripts, you can find different balanced breathing techniques to share with your clients through meditation sessions.

Script #30: Equal Breathing

This meditation is here to help you guide your clients through equal breathing, a breathwork technique that stabilizes the nervous system and promotes mental and emotional balance through focusing on even inhalations and exhalations. You can create a steady rhythm that encourages relaxation and clarity.

1. Find a comfortable position, either seated with your spine upright or lying down with your body fully supported.

2. Close your eyes or soften your gaze. Take a moment to check in with your body. Notice any areas of tension or any sensations that arise.

3. Without changing anything yet, simply observe your breath. Feel the natural rise and fall of your inhale and exhale.

4. Now, take a slow, deep breath in through your nose... and exhale fully through your mouth. Let yourself settle into stillness.

5. (Pause for 30 seconds.)

6. Begin the practice of equal breathing. The goal is to make the inhale and exhale the same length, creating a steady, calming rhythm.

    a. Inhale through your nose for a count of four...

    b. Exhale through your nose for a count of four...

7. Repeat:

    a. Inhale... 2... 3... 4...

    b. Exhale... 2... 3... 4...

8. Now, continue this pattern on your own, maintaining smooth, even breaths. Feel the steadiness in your breath, bringing steadiness to your mind.

9. (Pause for 3 minutes, guiding as needed.)

10. If it feels natural, you may begin to extend the count to five or six, lengthening the breath without strain.

11. (Pause for 1 minute.)

12. Release the breath pattern and return to your natural breathing. Notice how your body feels—perhaps there's a sense of ease, a quiet stillness.

13. Equal Breathing is a simple yet powerful tool that you can use at any time. Whether in moments of stress or simply to reconnect with yourself, this breathwork offers a pathway back to balance.

14. Take one final deep breath in... and a slow, gentle exhale. When you're ready, bring movement back to your fingers and toes and open your eyes.

Script #31: Box Breathing (4-4-4-4 Breathwork)

This technique is similar to equal breathing, where the inhale and exhale are of equal length. However, box breathing adds breath retention after both the inhale and the exhale. This extra step helps regulate the nervous system, enhance focus, and restore balance. While equal breathing creates a smooth, calming rhythm, box breathing offers deeper control over the breath, making it especially useful for building resilience to stress and improving focus.

1. Find a comfortable position, either seated with an upright spine or lying down in a relaxed posture. Gently close your eyes or soften your gaze. Take a moment to notice your breath, observing it without changing anything yet.

2. Now, take a deep breath in through your nose... and exhale fully through your mouth.

3. (Pause for 30 seconds.)

4. We will now begin box breathing, a structured breath pattern that follows an equal rhythm:

   a. Inhale for 4 seconds

   b. Hold the breath for 4 seconds

   c. Exhale for 4 seconds

   d. Hold again for 4 seconds

5. This balanced cycle regulates oxygen and carbon dioxide levels, signals safety to the nervous system, and creates a steady state of relaxation and alertness.

6. Let's begin:

   a. Inhale through your nose... 1... 2... 3... 4...

   b. Hold... 1... 2... 3... 4...

c. Exhale through your mouth... 1... 2... 3... 4...

d. Hold... 1... 2... 3... 4...

7. (Pause for 3 minutes, guiding as needed.)

8. Now, release the structured breath and return to your natural rhythm. Notice how you feel—perhaps steadier, centered, or calm.

9. Take one final deep breath in... and exhale slowly. When you're ready, bring movement back to your fingers and toes and gently open your eyes.

Script #32: Alternate Nostril Breathing

This meditation will guide you through alternate nostril breathing to help those you work with bring harmony to both hemispheres of the brain, promoting focus, clarity, and inner calm.

1. Find a comfortable seated position with your spine straight and shoulders relaxed. Gently rest your hands on your lap and take a few natural breaths, noticing the flow of air as it moves in and out of your body.

2. Close your eyes if that feels comfortable. Take a slow inhale through your nose... and exhale completely. Let go of any tension or distractions.

   a. Bring your right hand to your face. Use your thumb to gently close your right nostril.

   b. Inhale deeply through your left nostril... 1... 2... 3... 4...

   c. Now, close your left nostril with your ring finger and release your thumb.

   d. Exhale through your right nostril... 1... 2... 3... 4...

e.   Inhale through your right nostril... 1... 2... 3... 4...

f.   Close your right nostril and release your ring finger.

g.   Exhale through your left nostril... 1... 2... 3... 4...

h.   This completes one full cycle.

3.   Continue at your own pace, keeping the breath slow and steady. With each inhale, invite clarity. With each exhale, let go of tension.

4.   (Pause for 4 minutes, allowing time for breath cycles.)

5.   Gently lower your hand and return to natural breathing. Notice how you feel—perhaps lighter, calmer, or more centered.

6.   Take a final deep breath in... and a slow, full exhale. When you feel ready, open your eyes and return to the present moment, carrying this sense of balance with you.

Script #33: Humming Breath

This meditation works with humming breath, or Bhramari, a practice that uses sound and vibration to calm the nervous system.

1.   Find a comfortable seated position, ensuring your back is straight and your shoulders relaxed. Rest your hands gently on your lap. Close your eyes if that feels comfortable and begin by taking a deep inhale through your nose... and a long, steady exhale through your mouth.

2.   (Pause for 30 seconds.)

3.   Now, bring your attention to the sensation of your breath. Notice the rise and fall of your chest, the coolness of the air as you inhale, and the warmth as you exhale.

4.   We will now begin the humming breath.

a. Take a deep inhale through your nose... and as you exhale, softly hum, allowing the sound to vibrate through your body.

b. (Hum for 5–6 seconds, then pause.)

c. Again, inhale deeply... and exhale with a gentle, continuous hum.

5. (Pause for 4 minutes, guiding as needed.)

6. As you continue, feel the vibrations moving through your chest, your throat, and even your head. This sound connects you to your inner stillness, releasing tension and bringing a sense of peace.

7. (Pause for 1 minute.)

8. Release the humming and return to natural breathing. Observe how your body feels. Is there a sense of lightness or ease? Do you notice any shifts in your energy?

9. (Pause.)

10. Take one final deep breath in... and a slow, full exhale. When you feel ready, open your eyes, returning to the space around you.

Using Breath to Release Tension

Incorporating breathwork into meditation is an effective way to release physical tension and promote mental clarity. With these scripts, you can help your clients achieve tension release that is valuable for healing and feeling at peace.

Script #34: Diaphragmatic Breathing

Diaphragmatic breathing stands out as an incredible practice for achieving deep relaxation. Through encouraging the use of the diaphragm—our primary muscle of respiration—this technique boosts oxygen intake, aiding in both physical relaxation and tension release (Majsiak & Young, 2022).

This meditation uses diaphragmatic breathing to promote deep relaxation and enhance body awareness.

1. Find a comfortable seated or lying position. Allow your body to settle, and gently close your eyes or soften your gaze. Rest one hand on your abdomen and the other on your chest. Take a moment to feel the natural rhythm of your breath. Notice how your chest and belly move as you breathe in and out.

2. (Pause for 30 seconds to allow participants to observe and connect with the breath.)

3. Take a slow, deep breath in through your nose, feeling your belly expand. Exhale fully through your mouth, noticing the gentle release of tension.

4. (Pause.)

5. Focus on breathing deeply into your abdomen. As you inhale, let your belly rise rather than your chest. Imagine filling the lower part of your lungs, allowing your stomach to push outward.

   a. Inhale deeply for a count of four, feeling your abdomen rise.

   b. Pause briefly at the top of your breath.

   c. Exhale slowly for a count of four, allowing your belly to fall naturally.

6. Continue this pattern at your own pace. If your mind wanders, gently return your focus to the sensation of your belly expanding and contracting. With each breath, notice how the tension in your body eases away.

7. (Pause for 3-4 minutes, offering guidance every 60 seconds.)

8. Gradually return to your natural breathing pattern while keeping awareness on your diaphragm. Notice any difference in how your body feels—perhaps a sense of calm or increased relaxation.

9. (Pause.)

10. Take one final deep, slow diaphragmatic breath in… and exhale completely. When you feel ready, gently open your eyes and bring this sense of centered calm with you into the rest of your day.

Script #35: Intentional Sighing

Another useful technique is intentional sighing. A deep, purposeful sigh can almost reset the nervous system by facilitating stress alleviation by quickly shifting the body from a state of stress to calm (Your Headspace Mindfulness & Meditation Experts, 2023). Unlike incidental sighs, which are often unconscious, intentional sighing makes space for mindful engagement with the body's cues.

This meditation introduces intentional sighing as a method to quickly release built-up stress and shift the body from a state of tension to calm.

1. Find a comfortable position, sitting or lying down. Allow your body to relax, and softly close your eyes. Begin by taking a few deep, natural breaths. Notice any areas where tension might be present—your shoulders, jaw, or chest.

2. (Pause for 30 seconds, letting participants connect with breath and body tension.)

3. Now, we will practice intentional sighing.

   a. Inhale slowly and deeply through your nose, filling your lungs completely.

   b. At the top of your inhale, pause for a moment, then exhale forcefully through your mouth, as if you are letting out a long, purposeful sigh.

   c. Feel the tension lift with that exhale.

4. (Pause.)

5. Repeat this process:

   a. Inhale deeply for a count of four.

   b. Hold the breath for a brief moment.

   c. Exhale with a deliberate sigh for a count of six, releasing stress with the sound and sensation of your sigh.

6. Continue this pattern, allowing each sigh to clear away any residual stress or tightness. Notice how your body feels with each intentional, mindful exhale.

7. (Pause for 2-3 minutes, allowing time to continue the breathing cycle.)

8. Return to natural breathing, noticing the difference in your body after intentional sighing. Observe any reduction in tension and a greater sense of ease.

9. (Pause for 30 seconds to integrate the shift.)

10. Take one final deep breath in and exhale slowly, letting your body settle. When ready, open your eyes, carrying the calm and renewed energy of this practice into your daily life.

Script #36: Guided Visualization With Breath Focus

Guided visualizations paired with breath focus are a creative way to direct attention to tense regions within the body.

This meditation combines visualization with focused breathwork to help your clients direct their breath toward areas of tension in order to promote relaxation and enhanced body awareness.

1. Begin in a comfortable seated or lying position. Allow your eyes to close or gaze softly downward. Take a few deep, natural breaths, noticing any tight spots in your body, such as in your shoulders or back.

2. (Pause for 30 seconds to allow awareness to settle into the body.)

3. Imagine that with every inhale, you are drawing in fresh, calming air that reaches the areas where tension lingers. As you breathe in, focus your attention on a specific area of tightness—perhaps your shoulders or upper back.

4. Inhale slowly and deeply for a count of four, directing your breath into that area.

5. Hold briefly, feeling the air fill and ease the tension.

6. Exhale for a count of four, as if you are gently pushing out all the tension and discomfort.

7. Repeat this cycle, mentally focusing on different areas if you like. With each cycle, feel the tightness gradually ease as you direct your breath to where it is needed most.

8. (Pause for 2-3 minutes to continue breath-focused visualization on various areas of tension.)

9. Allow your breathing to return to its natural rhythm. Notice any improvements in how your body feels. Acknowledge the relaxation that has spread through the previously tense areas.

10. (Pause for 30 seconds.)

11. Take a final deep breath in and a long, unhurried exhale. When you're ready, gently open your eyes, carrying the sense of physical ease and mindfulness with you.

Script #37: Gentle Unwinding Breath

This technique encourages a slow, intentional unwinding of tension, allowing your clients to experience a deep sense of relaxation through their breath. It focuses on gradual, mindful exhalations to support a release of stress and tension in a more natural and organic way.

1. Begin by sitting comfortably or lying down in a relaxed position. Close your eyes or soften your gaze. Start by becoming aware of your body, noticing how you feel right now, without judgment. Take a moment to notice any areas of tension or discomfort, particularly in your shoulders, jaw, or stomach.

2. Take a few deep breaths to settle into the present moment. Inhale gently through your nose, feeling the air fill your lungs. Exhale slowly, releasing any initial tension as you soften with the breath. Repeat a couple of times, allowing your body to relax further with each exhalation.

3. Now, gently bring your focus to your breathing. With each inhale, imagine the air flowing in and bringing fresh energy into your body. When you exhale, instead of forcing the breath out, simply let the exhale happen naturally, like a slow release. There's no need to push or strain—just allow your body to relax and release any heaviness or tension with each exhale.

4. Feel how your body starts to unwind naturally as the air exits your lungs. Let go of any tightness, any buildup. You might notice that your shoulders drop slightly with each exhale or that your jaw softens. This is your body's way of responding to the breath—gently unwinding with each passing moment.

5. If any part of your body feels particularly tense, breathe into that area. Imagine the breath moving into the tension, and then, as you exhale, feel that area soften, like it's being gently released into the air. It's a natural, effortless sensation, with each exhalation letting go just a little more.

6. (Allow for 3-5 minutes of continued breathing with pauses.)

7. Continue breathing at a pace that feels comfortable, noticing how each exhale feels like a small wave of release, flowing through your body and out into the space around you. With each release, notice any emotional or physical relief, letting go of the weight you've been carrying.

8. Now, allow your breath to return to its natural rhythm. Feel a sense of lightness, ease, and calm spreading through your body. Notice how your body feels—perhaps a little more spacious, more relaxed, or simply more at ease.

9. Take one final, slow inhale, and exhale gently, letting your body settle deeply into this space of calm. When you feel ready, gently open your eyes, carrying with you the understanding that you can always return to this gentle unwinding breath whenever you need it.

10. Remember, this is a process, so be patient with yourself and others. Over time, the unwinding breath becomes more accessible, allowing a deeper release and greater relaxation each time you practice.

When exploring these techniques, it's important to be patient, especially for beginners. Starting gradually allows the nervous system to adjust without overwhelming feelings, which means that it's best to help those you work with start small. As they become more comfortable with these breathwork practices, gradually increase the duration and depth of your sessions.

Breath and Energy

Breath awareness is a powerful tool that connects us to our energy flow, which can impact our mental, emotional, and physical states. When you encourage those you work with to focus on their breath, they're participating in a process that influences how energy circulates within them.

Script #38: Energizing Breathwork

This meditation introduces energizing breathwork as a tool for increasing vitality and alertness. This script closely resembles a 1:2 breath ratio technique, which is a form of coherence or balancing breathwork with an energizing twist.

1. Find a comfortable seated position with an upright spine. Rest your hands on your thighs or in your lap. Close your eyes or soften your gaze, allowing yourself to arrive fully in this moment.

2. Begin by noticing the natural flow of your breath. Take a deep inhale through your nose, filling your lungs completely. Exhale fully through your mouth. Repeat once more, setting the foundation for this practice.

3. (Pause for 30 seconds to settle and prepare for energizing breath.)

4. Now, shift your focus to a rhythmic breath pattern:

   a. Inhale quickly and fully through your nose for a count of two.

   b. Exhale slowly and completely through your mouth for a count of four.

c. Feel the expansion in your lungs as each inhale draws in fresh energy and the release of any sluggishness as you exhale.

5. Continue this cycle at a steady pace. With every exhale, release any stagnation or fatigue. If comfortable, slightly increase the speed of your inhales while maintaining long, steady exhales.

6. (Pause for 2-3 minutes, inviting participants to continue breathing in this rhythm.)

7. Allow your breathing to return to a natural rhythm. Observe any shifts in your energy—perhaps a feeling of lightness, clarity, or readiness.

8. (Pause for 30 seconds to let the body integrate the shift.)

9. Take a final deep breath in, holding it for a brief moment before exhaling fully. Gently open your eyes, carrying this revitalized energy with you.

Script #39: Bellows Breath

Bellows breath is a vigorous practice that should be done on an empty stomach, with care to avoid overexertion. Clients who are pregnant, have high blood pressure, or are prone to dizziness should avoid this technique. After the practice, guide clients to pause in stillness for a few breaths before returning to a natural rhythm.

1. Close your eyes and begin to observe your natural breath. Take a moment to settle into the present, allowing any tension to slowly melt away.

2. Now, take a deep breath in through your nose, filling your lungs fully. As you exhale, force the air out sharply through your nose, making a strong and active exhale. Then, immediately inhale deeply and forcefully through your nose again, filling your lungs, and then exhale again with equal intensity.

3. Continue this breathing pattern—sharp, forceful inhales followed by equally strong exhales. Try to keep the rhythm steady, without pauses between breaths. The energy should feel lively and rhythmic, much like the bellows of a fire stoking a flame.

4. (Pause for 2 minutes of Bellows Breath with gentle guidance if necessary.)

5. Keep your attention focused on the flow of breath, allowing each cycle to invigorate your body and mind. Feel your energy shifting, your chest expanding, and your mind clearing with each breath. If you find your mind wandering, gently return your focus to the rhythm of the breath.

6. (Allow for 3-4 minutes of continued Bellows Breath, providing gentle guidance as needed.)

7. Now, slowly begin to reduce the intensity of your breath. Let your inhales and exhales soften naturally, returning to a gentle and easy rhythm. Take a few deep breaths to ground yourself in this sense of clarity and vitality.

8. When you're ready, gently open your eyes. Take a moment to notice the shift in your body and mind—perhaps feeling more awake, alert, and energized. Carry this clarity and focus with you as you move forward in your day.

Breath of Fire

Breath of Fire is a rapid, rhythmic breathing technique often used in Kundalini yoga. It involves short, quick exhales through the nose while the inhale happens naturally. This energizing breathwork boosts circulation, enhances focus, and strengthens the diaphragm. It is particularly beneficial for those looking to increase vitality and mental sharpness.

Script #40: Breath of Fire Breathing Exercise

Like bellows breath, this is an energizing and intense technique. It should be practiced on an empty stomach, ensuring clients do not overexert themselves. Those who are pregnant, have high blood pressure, or experience dizziness should refrain. Encourage clients to listen to their bodies and return to gentle breathing if needed.

1. Sit tall with a straight spine, resting your hands gently on your knees. Close your eyes or soften your gaze, bringing your awareness inward. Take a deep inhale through your nose, filling your lungs completely, feeling your ribs expand. Exhale fully through your mouth, releasing any tension or heaviness.

2. Now, bring your lips together and prepare for Breath of Fire. Begin with short, forceful exhalations through your nose, using your diaphragm to push the air out. The inhale will happen naturally in response—don't focus on it, just let it follow each sharp exhale. Imagine a rhythmic pumping of your breath, steady and consistent.

3. Start slowly, finding a pace that feels strong yet comfortable. Let's practice together:

    a. Exhale... Exhale... Exhale... Exhale...

4. Continue this rapid, even breath pattern. Your core remains engaged, and your spine stays long. If you're new to this practice, aim for a pace of one breath per second. As you build confidence, you can gradually increase the speed.

5. Maintain this for one minute to start. If it feels natural, extend the practice to two or even three minutes over time.

6. If at any point you feel lightheaded or unsteady, slow down or pause, returning to gentle, deep breaths.

7. (Allow 1-3 minutes as participants continue the Breath of Fire.)

8. When you're ready to close the practice, take a long, slow inhale through your nose... filling your lungs to capacity... and hold the breath for a few seconds, allowing the energy to circulate through your body. Then, exhale completely, releasing any remaining tension.

9. Return to your natural breath, soft and steady. Notice the subtle buzz of energy coursing through your system—a sense of revitalization, of inner warmth and clarity.

10. Take a final breath in... and a long, soothing exhale out. When you're ready, gently open your eyes, carrying this newfound energy and balance with you into the rest of your day.

Script #41: Lion's Breath

This breathwork technique helps clear stagnant energy, release pent-up stress, and invigorate the body by engaging both breath and movement. While fun and powerful for releasing tension, lion's breath is better suited for a more dynamic session or in a yoga class rather than a traditional meditation.

1. Find a comfortable seated position, either kneeling or cross-legged, with your spine tall. Rest your hands on your knees. Take a moment to settle in, closing your eyes if that feels natural.

2. Take a deep inhale through your nose, filling your belly. As you exhale, open your mouth wide, stick out your tongue, and let out a forceful "HA" sound—imagine you're a lion roaring out any tension or frustration.

3. Let's try this together:

   a. Inhale deeply through your nose... feel your lungs expand...

   b. Exhale powerfully through your mouth, tongue out, making a strong "HA" sound...

4. (Pause for 5 seconds.)

5. Let's repeat this for a few more rounds. With each exhale, visualize yourself releasing any stress, frustration, or heaviness.

    a. Inhale deeply...

    b. Exhale—roar it out...

6. (Repeat for 5–7 cycles.)

7. After your final round, return to a natural breath. Notice how your face, jaw, and shoulders feel—perhaps lighter, softer, more open.

8. (Pause to let participants observe their internal shift.)

9. Take one last deep breath in... and exhale gently. When you're ready, open your eyes and return to the present moment, feeling refreshed and renewed.

Integration of Breath Techniques

Each of these breathwork techniques serves a different purpose, and combining them can create a holistic approach to well-being. You can guide those you work with in experimenting with various methods based on their needs.

Encouraging those you work with to incorporate breathwork into daily life, whether as part of a morning routine or before bedtime, can lead to lasting benefits in stress management, self-awareness, and overall vitality. The breath is a powerful tool—one that, when harnessed with intention, has the ability to transform both mind and body.

Final Insights

Breathwork and meditation go hand in hand to create an incredible strategy for managing mental and emotional well-being. Throughout this chapter, we've explored various techniques like diaphragmatic breathing, equal breathing, and alternate nostril breathing that can enrich meditation practices. Integrating these methods means that you can guide your students or clients through an experience that promotes calmness and awareness.

What's remarkable about these techniques is their versatility and adaptability. You can introduce them in different settings to improve connections between the physical, mental, and emotional aspects of health. So, as you continue to explore these practices with your audience, remember that breath isn't just about oxygen; it's a technique for a more balanced, centered, and peaceful existence.

Chapter 6:

Scripts Targeting Emotional

Healing and Resilience

This chapter discusses how guided meditations designed to resolve emotional blockages and build resilience can be empowering and includes multiple scripts you can share directly with those you work with.

Healing Past Traumas

When looking at emotional healing and resilience, it's important to understand how past experiences shape our emotional responses. Our brains are like sponges when it comes to experiences, especially during childhood. These early encounters shape how we react emotionally as adults. Recognizing this connection can help those you work with see that their current emotional states often have deep-rooted origins.

Guided Inner Exploration Techniques

Guided inner exploration is a great technique for creating a safe, healing space. This technique lets participants explore their emotions in an environment free from judgment or fear. Inner exploration can also be a rehearsal space for emotional processing, where past traumas can be acknowledged without overwhelming distress. The practice aligns with timeline therapy principles, which emphasize reframing past experiences for positive change (Stuarttan, 2024).

1. Begin by finding a comfortable position, feeling fully supported in the space around you. Close your eyes or soften your gaze, taking a few deep breaths. With each inhale, draw in calm and peace, and with each exhale, release any tension or heaviness. Allow your breath to gently ground you in the present moment.

2. (Pause.)

3. As you settle, turn your attention inward. Notice any emotions or memories that arise naturally. Don't try to control or push them away—simply allow them to come up, observing them without judgment.

4. (Pause.)

5. If a feeling or memory surfaces, ask yourself, "What is this emotion trying to tell me?" or "What is the message beneath it?" Let the answer come with curiosity, without expectation or need to change anything. This is an exploration, not a moment to fix or judge.

6. (Pause here for 1.5-2 minutes to allow reflection.)

7. If a memory or past experience comes forward, simply observe it. You are in control, and nothing needs to overwhelm you. Know that you are safe in this moment, and this is an opportunity for understanding, not reliving.

8. (Pause.)

9. If the emotions feel heavy or intense, breathe deeply, allowing each exhale to bring release. Remember, you are here to explore, not to solve. Let the process unfold at its own pace.

10. (Pause.)

11. Reflect on how these emotions or experiences may have shaped your present moment. How do they influence your reactions

today? What patterns or insights arise? Acknowledge the ways these emotions may have served you, even if their role has changed over time.

12. (Pause here for 1-2 minutes to allow quiet inner reflection.)

13. Create space for new understanding. Release any judgment attached to the past and offer yourself compassion. Honor the growth you've made and the journey that has brought you here.

14. (Pause.)

15. Take a few more deep breaths, allowing the insights from this exploration to settle within you. With each breath, you invite a sense of empowerment, peace, and acceptance into your being.

16. (Pause for 1 minute to allow integration.)

17. When you're ready, gently bring your awareness back to the present. Take your time as you open your eyes, carrying this inner calm and newfound understanding with you into the rest of your day.

Affirmations for Healing

Affirmations are another necessary tool in the emotional healing process. These positive statements help counteract negative beliefs that may have formed due to past traumas. When clients repeat statements with intent, such as "I am worthy of love and compassion," they begin to internalize these truths. Affirmations work by replacing self-critical thoughts with nurturing ones in order to promote self-compassion. Clients gradually build a more positive self-image, reflecting their inherent value rather than their perceived flaws. This practice aligns with findings on mindfulness meditation, which enhances psychological well-being through focused mental exercises (Keng et al., 2011).

Script #43: Reclaiming Your Truth

1. Find a relaxed position. Let your body settle, releasing any tension. Close your eyes if you feel comfortable, or soften your gaze. Take a slow breath in, filling your lungs with calm, then exhale gently, releasing any weight you may be carrying.

2. (Pause for 30 seconds.)

3. Now, bring your awareness to your heart center. This is your inner truth—your deepest, most authentic self. Today, we will nurture this truth with affirmations, allowing them to take root within you.

4. (Pause.)

5. As you breathe in, silently or aloud, repeat: "I am worthy of love and compassion."

6. Feel the words settle into your body. Let them replace any doubts, any old narratives that no longer serve you.

7. (Pause for 30 seconds to absorb the affirmation.)

8. With your next breath, say: "I honor my journey and trust my healing process."

9. Picture these words wrapping around you like a protective embrace, reinforcing your strength.

10. (Pause for 30 seconds.)

11. Another deep inhale, and now: "I release self-judgment and welcome self-acceptance."

12. Let any tension melt away as these words anchor within you, reshaping the way you see yourself.

13. (Pause for 30 seconds.)

14. Now, in your own time, create a personal affirmation—one that speaks directly to your heart. Say it with conviction, allowing it to become part of your truth.

15. (Pause for 30 seconds to 1 minute for reflection and recitation.)

16. As this meditation comes to a close, take a final deep breath. Inhale self-compassion. Exhale anything that no longer serves you. Gently bring awareness back to your surroundings. Wiggle your fingers, roll your shoulders, and when you're ready, open your eyes.

17. (Pause.)

18. Carry these affirmations with you. They are not just words—they are seeds of transformation, growing stronger each time you return to them.

Understanding Emotional Triggers

Understanding emotional triggers tied to past experiences is necessary to break cycles of pain. As your clients uncover these triggers, they gain awareness of their automatic responses and can choose healthier reactions. Imagining past events within a safe mental space provides clarity because it reveals patterns that contribute to emotional blockages. In turn, this exploration encourages cognitive restructuring so that practitioners can replace outdated beliefs with empowering ones.

Script #44: Rewriting the Story

1. Settle into a comfortable position, feeling the surface beneath you supporting your body. Close your eyes, if that feels safe, and take a slow, steady breath in... then exhale, releasing any tension.

2. (Pause for 30 seconds.)

3. Now, bring your awareness to a place within your mind—a space that feels safe, protected, and free from judgment. It may be a quiet forest, a warm sunlit room, or a place from your past that brought you comfort. Allow yourself to settle here.

4. (Pause.)

5. In this space, imagine a small pool of water before you. The surface is still and reflective. This pool holds glimpses of your past—moments that shaped you, moments that may still carry weight within you. As you gaze into the water, a ripple forms, and an image begins to appear—a memory connected to an emotional trigger.

6. (Pause 30 seconds. Allow the memory to arise.)

7. Observe this memory as if watching a scene unfold on a screen. You are not inside the moment; you are simply witnessing it. Notice the details—where you are, what is happening, how your body feels. Allow yourself to acknowledge the emotions tied to this moment, without judgment or resistance.

8. (Pause 1-1.5 minutes to fully observe and acknowledge the scene.)

9. Now, take a slow breath in and step closer to this scene—not to relive it, but to rewrite it. Imagine yourself as you are now, with the wisdom and strength you have gained. See yourself stepping into this memory, gently placing a hand on the shoulder of your past self.

10. (Pause.)

11. What do you want to say to yourself? What does this version of you need to hear? Maybe it's reassurance. Maybe it's permission to let go. Maybe it's simply, "You are safe now. You are not defined by this moment."

12. (Pause for 1 minute for emotional dialogue.)

13. Watch as this version of you absorbs these words, softening, finding ease. The weight of the memory shifts. The narrative begins to change. It no longer holds power over you in the same way. It is part of your past, but it does not dictate your future.

14. (Pause 30 seconds.)

15. As the image fades, return your focus to the present. Breathe in deeply, anchoring yourself in this moment. Exhale, releasing what no longer serves you.

16. (Pause.)

17. When you are ready, gently wiggle your fingers, roll your shoulders, and open your eyes. Carry this clarity with you. You are not bound to old patterns. You have the power to rewrite your story.

Guided meditations using these techniques encourage participants to meet their emotions with curiosity and compassion. They learn to invite emotions in, observe them without judgment, and let them pass naturally. Doing so improves emotional resilience by showing participants that their feelings don't define them; instead, they possess the strength to navigate them. Implementing affirmations into these meditations helps create a mindset rooted in self-love by dismantling negative self-talk and planting seeds of positivity.

Building Emotional Strength

For those looking to develop emotional strength and resilience, focused meditation practices can be a big help. They make it far easier to bounce back from tricky situations, and beyond that, they encourage healing. At the heart of this practice lies an understanding of what makes someone resilient. Emotional resilience encompasses traits such as adaptability, optimism, and a robust sense of self-awareness. Adaptable people can fluidly move through life's changes without losing their balance, while optimists find the silver lining in nearly every cloud. Recognizing these traits in oneself can be the first step toward developing greater resilience.

Empowerment Meditations

Meditation, particularly empowerment meditations, helps with internalizing states of personal strength and success. This meditative practice encourages participants to imagine themselves achieving goals, overcoming obstacles, and embodying strength. Mentally rehearsing these scenarios is a way for participants to start to believe in their capabilities, which turns theoretical strength into something tangible. For example, a simple empowerment meditation might involve picturing a past success that allows the participant to relive the associated feelings of achievement and confidence. Repeated sessions enable this sense of success to embed itself into one's psyche, making resilience a natural response rather than a forced effort.

Script #45: Empowering Strength

1. Find a comfortable position. Allow your body to settle, releasing any tension as you gently close your eyes or soften your gaze. Take a deep, steady breath in... hold for a moment... then exhale slowly, letting go of any doubts or distractions.

2. (Pause.)

3. Now, bring to mind a moment in your life when you felt strong. It may be a time you overcame an obstacle, accomplished a goal, or stood firm in your truth. It does not have to be grand—perhaps it was a small victory that filled you with pride.

4. (Pause for 30 seconds to recall the memory.)

5. See this moment clearly. Where were you? What did you feel in your body? The confidence in your stance, the ease in your

breath, the certainty in your heart. Let that feeling expand within you, as if you are reliving it now.

6. (Pause for 30 seconds to 1 minute.)

7. As you inhale, imagine drawing this strength deeper into your core. Feel it settle into your bones, your muscles, your very being. With each breath, this power becomes more tangible— no longer just a memory, but a part of who you are.

8. (Pause for 30 seconds to breath and embody the strength.)

9. Now, imagine a challenge before you—something that once felt too great to overcome. But this time, you approach it with the strength you just reclaimed. See yourself navigating it with clarity, resilience, and determination. Notice how your body carries this confidence, how your mind remains steady. You are not just envisioning success—you are embodying it.

10. (Pause 1 minute for visualization.)

11. Hold onto this feeling. Let it root within you, so deep that no external force can shake it. You are strong. You are capable. You are already the person who can overcome, who can achieve, who can thrive.

12. (Pause 30 seconds to affirm and integrate.)

13. Take a deep breath in, locking in this empowerment. Exhale slowly, knowing that this strength is always within you.

14. (Pause.)

15. When you are ready, begin to bring awareness back to your body. Step forward with the unwavering knowledge that you are more powerful than you have ever realized.

Setting Personal Boundaries

Furthermore, setting personal boundaries is necessary for self-advocacy and maintaining emotional health. Meditation can help establish these boundaries by creating a deeper understanding of personal limits and needs. In a meditative state, participants can reflect on instances where boundaries were breached and how that felt. They can mentally rehearse how they wish to react in future boundary-testing situations. You can incorporate these elements into any meditation script I've shared, based on the needs of the individuals you work with.

Resilience Building

Reflecting on past experiences of resilience can reinforce the understanding that they have the tools needed to handle adversity. It's about connecting past achievements with future challenges, thus reaffirming their ability to face new trials with courage.

Combining Creativity

Another wonderful approach involves combining creativity with meditation.

Script #46: Canvas of the Mind

1. Settle into a comfortable position. Let your body relax, your breath finding its own natural rhythm. Close your eyes if you wish, or simply soften your gaze. There is no right or wrong way to be here—only presence.

2. (Pause for 30 seconds to settle.)

3. Now, see a vast, open space before you. It could be a canvas, a page, an instrument waiting for your touch. This space is yours—boundless, free of judgment, ready to hold whatever needs to emerge.

4. With your next inhale, see a color forming in your mind. It may be soft and gentle, or bold and vivid. This color carries an emotion—one that is present within you. Let it flow onto the canvas, spreading in any way it wishes. No control, no expectation. Simply movement, expression.

5. (Pause for 45 seconds.)

6. Now, another color appears, weaving into the first. It shifts, expands, and tells a story. With each breath, more shades emerge, forming patterns, images, or abstract shapes—whatever arises naturally. Let these colors speak for you, releasing what words cannot capture.

7. (Pause for 30 seconds to visualize.)

8. If you feel drawn to sound, imagine the colors transforming into music. A rhythm begins—perhaps a steady pulse or a gentle melody. Feel it resonate through your body, vibrating in your fingertips, your chest, your breath.

9. Or perhaps you sense words forming, a stream of thoughts flowing like ink onto a page. They do not need to make sense. Let them arrive as they wish, raw and unfiltered.

10. (Pause 45-60 seconds for individual expression.)

11. This is a space where nothing is judged, nothing is held back. Only creation, only release.

12. Pause for a moment, taking in what you have created.

13. (Pause for 1 minute, allowing deep reflection and observation.)

14. Observe without analyzing. What emotions have taken form? What has shifted within you?

15. (Pause for 30 seconds.)

16. Now, with your next inhale, imagine the colors, sounds, or words gently settling—absorbing into you, not as weight, but as understanding. Exhale gently. You are lighter now, freer.

17. Take one more deep breath in, holding this feeling of expression and release. Exhale, knowing that creativity is always within you, waiting to be a refuge, a guide, a voice.

18. (Pause.)

19. When you are ready, return to your surroundings. Carry this creative energy with you, knowing that every moment is a blank canvas, ready for your truth.

Developing Emotional Intelligence

Emotional intelligence involves understanding and managing our emotions, and developing this ability can be incredibly rewarding.

Recognizing Emotions

First, let's explore how clients can learn to recognize and understand their own emotions using mindfulness. Mindfulness emphasizes paying attention to the present moment without judgment, and this practice can help emotional patterns and signals become clearer. When people engage in mindfulness, they become more aware of their emotions as they arise, rather than getting swept away by them. For example, during meditation, guiding clients to notice where they feel tension or ease in their bodies when experiencing different emotions can be enlightening. This heightened awareness aids in understanding one's emotional triggers and patterns to create more balanced reactions to challenges.

Script #47: Listening to Your Inner Landscape

1. Take a moment to find a comfortable position. Allow your body to settle, releasing any tension you may be holding. Let your hands rest gently, and your shoulders soften. Take a slow, steady breath in... and exhale at your own pace.

2. (Pause for 30 seconds to settle into stillness.)

3. Now, bring your awareness inward. There is no need to change anything—simply observe. Like a quiet witness, notice the sensations within you.

4. As you breathe in, scan your body from head to toe. Where do you feel ease? Where do you feel tension? Is there warmth, coolness, stillness? Every sensation is a message, an invitation to understand yourself more deeply.

5. (Pause for 1 minute to allow a full scan.)

6. Now, gently bring to mind an emotion that has been present for you recently. It may be subtle or strong, comfortable or challenging. Whatever arises, allow it space to exist without pushing it away or clinging to it.

7. (Pause for 30 seconds to reflect on the emotion.)

8. Where does this emotion live in your body? Is it a tightness in your chest, a flutter in your stomach, a weight in your shoulders? Observe it without judgment—only curiosity.

9. Breathe into this sensation. Not to force it away, but to acknowledge it, to give it space to soften and unfold. Emotions are like waves; they rise, they crest, they pass. You are the observer, standing at the shore, watching with gentle awareness.

10. (Pause for 1 minute, allowing for a few mindful breaths and reflection.)

11. Now, imagine asking this emotion a question: What do you need me to know? Listen. Not with expectation, but with openness. Perhaps an answer comes as a word, an image, or simply a feeling. Trust whatever arises.

12. (Allow for 1-2 minutes of quiet listening.)

13. Take another deep breath in, allowing this moment of understanding to settle within you. Exhale, releasing any resistance.

14. As you come to a close, gently bring your awareness back to your surroundings. Move your fingers, stretch your body, and when you're ready, open your eyes. Remember—your emotions are not obstacles. They are guides, always inviting you to listen, to understand, and to respond with balance and clarity.

Empathy Development

Once those you work with deepen their understanding of their emotions, developing empathy becomes the next step. Empathy allows people to connect with others on a deeper level, and meditation can be a great way to improve this ability. Guiding your clients in meditations that focus on imagining themselves in another person's shoes can greatly expand their empathetic capacity.

Script #48: Stepping Into Another's World

1. Find a comfortable position and allow your body to settle. Close your eyes or soften your gaze. Take a deep breath in... and exhale slowly. Let go of any distractions, allowing yourself to be fully present in this moment.

2. (Pause for 30 seconds.)

3. Now, bring to mind someone you have interacted with recently. It could be a loved one, a colleague, or a stranger in

passing. Hold their image gently in your mind, as if you are sitting across from them, seeing them clearly.

4. (Pause for 30 seconds to visualize the person.)

5. Without judgment, begin to wonder what they might have been feeling in that moment? Was there joy in their voice? Hesitation in their posture? Did their energy seem light or heavy? Simply observe, without assuming, without needing to be right.

6. (Pause for 30-45 seconds to reflect on their emotions.)

7. Now, imagine stepping into their experience. If they were carrying stress, what might that feel like in their body? If they were joyful, how did that warmth spread through them? Move beyond their actions and into their emotions. Let yourself sit with their perspective, even if it is different from your own.

8. (Pause 1-2 minutes to deepen empathy and perspective.)

9. Take a slow, deep breath in... and as you exhale, send them a silent offering of understanding. A wish for ease, for peace, for whatever they may need. Feel this connection between you— not as something forced, but as a quiet recognition of shared human experience.

10. (Pause for 30-45 seconds to sit in this connection.)

11. As you breathe, notice what has shifted within you. Has your heart softened? Has your mind expanded? Hold onto this awareness, this openness.

12. (Pause.)

13. Now, gently return to yourself. Feel your own body, your own breath. You are here, grounded, but carrying with you a deeper understanding of the emotions that move through all of us.

14. (Pause for 30 seconds before closing the meditation.)

15. Take one final breath in… and as you exhale, let a sense of connection remain with you. When you're ready, bring your awareness back to the room. Move your fingers, stretch your body, and open your eyes.

16. Empathy is not about fixing or solving—it is about witnessing, about being present with another's truth. And the more we practice, the more naturally it becomes a part of us.

Building Healthy Relationships

Building healthy relationships is another aspect of emotional intelligence, and role-playing communication skills in meditation can make a significant difference. During meditation sessions, inviting your participants to imagine conversations where they practice active listening and assertive communication encourages them to rehearse real-life scenarios in a safe environment. Furthermore, these sessions can address common communication barriers, which helps participants identify areas for improvement and growth (Schumacher, 2024).

Script #49: The Art of Connection

1. Find a comfortable position and take a slow, deep breath in. Feel the air fill your lungs, then exhale gently, releasing any tension. Let your shoulders drop, your hands rest easily, and your breath settle into a natural rhythm.

2. (Pause for 30 seconds.)

3. Now, bring to mind a conversation you need to have. It could be with a loved one, a colleague, or someone with whom communication has been challenging. Picture this person sitting across from you, their presence steady and open.

4. (Pause for 30 seconds to visualize this person.)

5. As you inhale, imagine yourself grounded, calm, and present. There is no rush—only space to express yourself clearly. As

you exhale, feel any tension dissolve, leaving behind a sense of confidence and ease.

6. Now, picture yourself speaking. Your voice is steady, your words intentional. What do you need to say? How do you wish to be understood? Take a moment to articulate your thoughts, knowing that you are expressing yourself with clarity and respect.

7. (Pause for 45-60 seconds.)

8. Now, imagine the other person responding—not just with words, but with their body language, their energy. How are they receiving your message? Are they listening, reflecting, understanding? Watch their expression, notice their emotions.

9. (Pause for 30 seconds to reflect on the response.)

10. Now, shift your focus to listening. See yourself fully engaged, giving them space to speak. Feel yourself absorbing their words, not just hearing them but truly understanding. You are present, receptive, and patient.

11. If there is conflict, imagine responding with curiosity instead of defensiveness. If there is a misunderstanding, envision yourself asking for clarity rather than assuming. See the conversation flowing with mutual respect, a balanced exchange of thoughts and emotions.

12. (Pause for 30-45 seconds.)

13. Take another deep breath in, letting this experience settle within you. As you exhale, carry forward this feeling of confidence, presence, and openness.

14. Every conversation is an opportunity—not just to speak, but to connect. And each time you practice, you strengthen your ability to communicate with both honesty and understanding.

For holistic practitioners, life coaches, therapists, yoga teachers, and others looking to integrate these approaches, it's important to tailor these practices to meet individual needs. Each participant may respond differently to various methods, so flexibility and adaptability in sharing these scripts are necessary. Encouraging your participants to keep an open mind and try out different techniques will improve their journey toward emotional intelligence.

The Art of Surrender

Surrender is a powerful concept often misunderstood in the process of gaining emotional healing and resilience. It doesn't mean resignation or giving up, but rather embracing the reality of what we cannot change and letting go of the resistance that causes ongoing suffering. It involves recognizing our emotions and experiences as they are without judgment or avoidance. This allows us to move forward with clarity and peace.

Script #50: Letting Go With the Wind

1. Settle into a position that feels the most relaxed for you in this moment. Close your eyes if you feel comfortable, or simply soften your gaze. Take a deep breath in through your nose... and exhale slowly through your mouth. Let your shoulders drop, your hands rest gently, and your breath settle into a natural rhythm.

2. (Pause for 30 seconds to settle.)

3. Imagine yourself standing in a quiet forest during autumn. The air is crisp and refreshing, carrying the gentle scent of earth and fallen leaves. Sunlight filters through the branches, casting golden patterns on the ground.

4. (Pause.)

5. As you breathe, notice the trees around you—strong, steady, yet effortlessly releasing their leaves. They do not cling to what

is ready to fall. They simply let go, trusting the wind to carry each leaf where it needs to go.

6. Now, picture yourself holding a leaf in your hand. This leaf represents something you have been carrying—a worry, a regret, a lingering thought. Take a moment to acknowledge it. There is no need to judge it or push it away. Just notice it, as it is.

7. (Pause for 30 seconds.)

8. When you feel ready, open your palm and allow the wind to lift the leaf from your hand. Watch as it dances through the air, drifting and twirling, until it disappears into the sky. There is no effort, no force—only release.

9. (Pause for 30 seconds to imagine movement of the leaf.)

10. One by one, gather more leaves. Each one holds a different thought, feeling, or burden you are ready to let go of. With each exhale, allow another leaf to rise and float away, carried effortlessly by the breeze.

11. (Pause for 1-2 minutes, allowing time for multiple releases.)

12. As the trees continue to release their leaves around you, feel a deep sense of trust within yourself—trust that you, too, can let go. Not by forcing, but by allowing.

13. Take a few more breaths in this space, feeling lighter with each release. Notice what remains—the quiet, the openness, the gentle rhythm of your breath.

14. (Pause for 30 seconds.)

15. When you are ready, bring awareness back to your body. Wiggle your fingers, shift your posture slightly, and take a final deep inhale. As you exhale, know that you can return to this place whenever you need. Open your eyes when you feel ready, carrying this sense of ease with you.

Script #51: The Bonfire of Release

1. Close your eyes and take a deep, steady breath in. Feel the air move through your body, filling you with presence. As you exhale, imagine releasing a small weight—just enough to begin feeling lighter.

2. (Pause for 30 seconds to let participants settle and fully engage the imagery.)

3. Now, picture yourself standing in an open clearing under a vast night sky. Above you, stars stretch endlessly, shimmering with quiet wisdom. The air is crisp and still, carrying the scent of earth and woodsmoke. Before you, a bonfire glows, its flames dancing in golden waves, warm but not overwhelming. This fire is ancient, wise, and ready to receive whatever you are prepared to release.

4. (Pause for 45 seconds, letting the scene form with sensory detail.)

5. Take a moment to notice the weight you have been carrying— the burdens of past wounds, the echoes of self-doubt, the worries that sit heavy in your chest. There is no need to judge them, only to acknowledge their presence.

6. (Pause for 45 seconds to reflect on what is being carried.)

7. Now, look beside you. There is a small bundle of twigs, each one representing something you are ready to let go of. You pick one up, feeling its rough texture in your hand. This twig holds an old hurt, something you have carried for too long. With a deep breath, step forward and gently place it into the fire.

8. (Pause.)

9. Watch as the flames consume it, curling around it, transforming it into light and warmth. You do not have to hold it anymore.

10. (Pause for 30 seconds.)

11. One by one, pick up the twigs and release them into the fire. Maybe one holds a lingering resentment, another a fear that no longer serves you. With each release, feel the lightness growing within you, as though space is opening where heaviness once lived.

12. (Allow 2-3 minutes for several symbolic releases.)

13. Now, simply sit by the fire. Feel its warmth, not as something to fear, but as something cleansing, something renewing. This fire does not destroy; it transforms. Whatever you have released is not lost—it is becoming something new, something freer.

14. (Pause 1 minute.)

15. Breathe deeply, feeling this newfound space within you. Sit in this moment of lightness, of clarity, of release.

16. (Pause for 1-2 minutes.)

17. When you are ready, begin to bring your awareness back. The fire will always be here when you need it. Take one last deep, cleansing breath. As you exhale, gently open your eyes.

18. You are lighter now. You have made space for peace.

Creating Release Rituals

Creating rituals for symbolic emotional release can also be incredibly supportive. Rituals grounded in nature or utilizing specific objects can be physical representations of letting go. This could be as simple as writing down negative emotions on pieces of paper and burning them in a fire, symbolizing transformation and renewal. Another way is to use natural elements like water to wash away stress and sadness; standing by a stream and watching leaves being carried away by the currents, like negative thoughts, can be profoundly healing. These rituals turn abstract feelings into concrete actions, which mark the transition from holding on to freeing oneself. You can help your participants work with release rituals during the above meditations—or any others—as suited for individual needs.

Letting go of negative emotions or experiences does not happen overnight; it's a gradual process that can be encouraged through consistent practice and support.

Cultivating Joy and Positivity

Another important step toward emotional healing and resilience is gaining a sense of joy and positivity in one's life—which means that meditations focused on joy and positivity can be incredible for those you work with. While fleeting moments of happiness arise naturally, the ability to sustain joy requires intentional practice. This section explores various techniques for enhancing joy and includes targeted guided meditation scripts that you can use with your clients.

Understanding Joy

True joy is rooted in presence. Unlike happiness, which often depends on external circumstances, joy is a deeper, more stable emotion that can be cultivated regardless of life's challenges. When your clients learn to recognize and invite joy into their lives, they create a lasting internal resource that supports resilience and emotional well-being.

Script #52: Awaken Your Inner Joy

1. Close your eyes and take a slow, steady breath in. Feel your ribs gently expand and your body relax into the present moment. As you exhale, release any heaviness, softening your jaw, your shoulders, and your hands.

2. (Pause for 30 seconds.)

3. Now, think of a time when you felt a spark of pure joy—a laugh shared with a friend, the rush of wind on a carefree day, or the quiet peace of something simple but beautiful. Let the memory come naturally, without searching too hard.

4. (Allow 1 minute for the memory to surface.)

5. Step into the feeling, not the image. Notice the way your body responds—perhaps a lightness in your chest, a soft smile on your lips, or a quiet hum of happiness deep within. Focus on these physical sensations, allowing them to build and spread with each breath.

6. (Pause 1 minute.)

7. As you inhale, invite this sense of joy to grow—a tingle in your fingertips, a gentle pulse in your heart. With every exhale, let it ripple through you, filling the empty spaces inside.

8. (Pause 1 minute.)

9. Now, place your hands over your heart. Take a moment to silently remind yourself: Joy lives within me. It's always here, waiting to rise.

10. (Pause for 45 seconds to let the affirmation resonate.)

11. Linger in this feeling for a few more breaths. Let it anchor itself in your body, like a quiet rhythm you can return to at any time.

12. (Pause for a few slow breaths.)

13. When you're ready, gently open your eyes. Carry this spark of joy with you—not as a glowing light, but as a steady presence, always just beneath the surface.

Cultivating Appreciation

Appreciation shifts focus from what is lacking to what is abundant. Regular appreciation practices can rewire the brain to notice and appreciate positive experiences, which makes joy more accessible. Encouraging participants to engage in appreciation-focused meditations helps ground their awareness in appreciation rather than scarcity.

Script #53: Embracing Life's Blessings

1. Begin by settling into a comfortable position and taking a deep, steady breath in. Exhale slowly, allowing your body to relax more deeply with each breath.

2. (Pause for 30 seconds to allow the body to settle.)

3. Now, think of a moment that brings you peace—perhaps the comfort of your favorite chair, the smile of a loved one, or a quiet walk in nature. Let yourself fully immerse in this memory, savoring how it feels in your body.

4. (Pause for 45 seconds.)

5. As you reflect on this moment, notice the warmth it brings. It may be a sense of calm in your heart, a gentle smile on your face, or a softening in your shoulders. Allow these sensations to fill your being, letting them expand with every breath.

6. (Pause for 30 seconds. Let participants breath with the sensation.)

7. Now, bring to mind another experience—maybe a small moment of kindness, something you've received or shared with someone else. Feel the positive energy from that exchange, knowing how it has enriched your life.

8. (Pause for 45 seconds.)

9. Continue to think of moments like these—each one adding to the feeling of fullness within you. With every breath, let the appreciation for these experiences deepen, knowing that they are a part of you, shaping who you are.

10. (Pause for 1 minute, allowing time for a few more moments to come to mind.)

11. Take one final deep breath, letting this sense of fullness and contentment settle deeply in your heart. When you're ready, gently bring your awareness back to the present moment, gently moving your fingers and toes, and open your eyes, carrying this peaceful feeling with you.

Script #54: The Garden of Joy

1. Close your eyes and take a deep breath. Let your body relax as you inhale and exhale any tension you may be holding.

2. (Pause to allow the body to fully settle.)

3. In your mind's eye, visualize that you're walking along a path in nature, where the air is fresh and smells faintly of new flower blossoms. Birds sing softly in the distance, and a gentle breeze moves through the leaves around you.

4. (Pause for 45 seconds to let participants build the scene.)

5. Ahead, you see a beautiful garden—one that exists just for you. Every plant, every color, every sound has been placed here to bring you joy. Step into the garden and take a moment to explore. What colors stand out? What scents fill the air? Notice the way the earth feels beneath your feet.

6. (Pause 1 minute.)

7. As you walk, imagine that each step deepens your sense of joy. You reach out and touch a flower, feeling its softness, its life. This garden is a reflection of your own inner joy, a space that always exists within you.

8. (Pause for 45 seconds.)

9. Take a moment to sit on a bench, breathing in the beauty around you. Whisper to yourself: Joy is always within reach.

10. (Pause for 30 seconds.)

11. When you're ready, begin to walk back along the path, knowing you can return here anytime. Slowly bring awareness to your body and open your eyes.

Spreading Positivity

When joy is cultivated, it naturally extends outward. Encouraging your clients to share their positive energy with others deepens their own sense of happiness. Acts of kindness, compassion, and mindful presence create ripples of positivity that not only uplift them as individuals but also strengthen their connections with others.

Script #55: Sending Kindness and Compassion to Others

1. Find a comfortable position where you feel solid and at ease. Let go of any distractions and settle into this moment.

2. (Pause for 30 seconds.)

3. Shift your attention to the feelings of kindness and compassion within you. With every inhale, feel these qualities grow. With each exhale, send that energy outward, imagining it expanding into the world.

4. (Pause for 45 seconds.)

5. Now, bring to mind someone you care about—a friend, family member, or someone close to you. Without saying anything out loud, silently wish them well. Send them your compassion, wishing them peace, health, and happiness. Picture them

receiving your positive intentions and feel your connection to them.

6. (Pause 1 minute.)

7. Next, think of someone you don't know well, perhaps a colleague or even a stranger. Send them your silent well wishes. Wish them happiness, strength, and well-being. Acknowledge that, like everyone, they have their own challenges and also deserve peace.

8. (Pause 1 minute.)

9. Finally, extend your compassion to all people, everywhere. Wish peace, health, and strength for everyone, no matter their circumstances. Feel the power of your intention reaching out, connecting you to others through the shared experience of humanity.

10. (Pause 1-2 minutes.)

11. Take a deep breath, feeling the strength of this connection. Let it settle, knowing that the compassion you send out also benefits you.

12. (Pause 30-45 seconds to fully absorb the feeling.)

13. Slowly open your eyes, and carry this sense of peace and compassion with you as you move through your day.

Bringing It All Together

This chapter took you through how various meditations can be used to address emotional blockages and build resilience for your clients—techniques such as surrender, affirmations, and creativity—each playing a unique role in emotional healing.

Our discussion also shows the importance of understanding past traumas and how they influence present emotional responses. Through mindful exploration, clients can uncover personal triggers, gain new insights, and learn healthier reactions. Guided meditations encourage curiosity and compassion that help participants meet their emotions without fear and judgment.

Chapter 7:

Meditations for Enhancing

Personal Self-Care

Enhancing personal self-care through meditation means creating a deeper connection with oneself, which is necessary for anyone you work with who often prioritizes others' needs over their own. For these individuals, taking the time to integrate meditation into their daily routines helps rejuvenate both body and mind. Turning inward and focusing on personal well-being means that you can help participants replenish their energy reserves.

Morning Meditation for Clarity and Intentions

Starting the day with clarity and intention can significantly impact the mental and emotional well-being of those you work with. Sharing these concepts and scripts with your participants can amplify their sense of wellness and ensure they start their day off positively.

Clarity and Grounding

The first step toward achieving this morning clarity is teaching participants to find a comfortable position to ground themselves. This process involves creating an environment conducive to meditation—one that is tranquil and free from distractions. Encourage them to either sit or lie down in a posture that feels stable and supportive. Whether it's sitting cross-legged on the floor or reclining on a cushioned chair, the key is finding a space where they feel both relaxed and alert. Then, you can share the following grounding meditation with them, which is perfect for starting the day off on a positive, present-focused note.

Script #56: Morning Grounding Meditation

1. Begin by settling into a position that feels supportive and steady. Whether you're sitting upright or lying down, allow your body to feel at ease while remaining aware. Take a slow, deep breath in through your nose, letting the air expand your ribs and belly. Hold for a moment. Now, exhale through your mouth, releasing any lingering tension.

2. (Pause.)

3. As you breathe naturally, bring your attention to the sensation of your body making contact with the surface beneath you. Feel the stability of the ground, the support of your seat, and the gentle weight of your body resting. With each breath, imagine yourself becoming more connected to this moment—steady, present, and awake.

4. (Pause for 45 seconds to deepen the connection.)

5. Now, bring your awareness to the rhythm of your breath. Notice how it moves through you effortlessly, steady and natural. Each inhale creates space, and each exhale clears away anything unnecessary—stiffness, grogginess, mental clutter. Let your breath anchor you, steadying your thoughts like a calm surface of water.

6. (Pause for 1-2 minutes.)

7. Shift your awareness to your surroundings. Even with your eyes closed, notice the subtle sounds around you—the distant hum of morning, the quiet stillness of the space you're in. Let these sounds exist without pulling your attention away. They simply remind you that the world is waking up with you, and you are part of it.

8. (Pause for 1-2 minutes.)

9. Take a moment to set an intention for the day ahead. It can be a single word—focus, ease, patience—or a simple phrase: "I move through today with clarity and purpose. Let this intention settle into your being, carried with each breath."

10. (Pause for 1 minute.)

11. When you're ready, gently wiggle your fingers and toes, bringing movement back into your body. Take one final, deep inhale, filling yourself with fresh energy, and exhale fully. Slowly open your eyes, carrying this sense of grounding and clarity into your day.

Inner Preparation for Your Day Ahead

Script #57: Stepping Into Your Day With Purpose

1. Begin by settling into a comfortable position, either seated or lying down. Close your eyes and take a deep breath in, feeling the air expand your chest and belly. Hold for a moment, then exhale slowly, releasing any tension. Take another deep breath, letting it center you in this moment.

2. (Pause.)

3. Now, imagine yourself standing at the entrance of a peaceful path, stretching ahead of you. The air is crisp, the surroundings calm. This path represents your day ahead—filled with possibility, steady and open.

4. (Pause for 30 seconds to allow the visualization.)

5. As you take your first step forward, picture the events of your day unfolding with ease. See yourself moving through each moment with confidence and clarity. Whether it's

conversations, tasks, or challenges, imagine yourself handling everything with grace and purpose.

6. (Pause for 1-1.5 minutes.)

7. With each step, feel a sense of calm and assurance growing within you. Notice how smoothly things fall into place—decisions come easily, interactions feel natural, and you meet each situation with a clear mind. There's no rush, no pressure—only steady movement forward.

8. (Pause for 1 minute.)

9. Now, focus on the emotions you want to carry through your day. Perhaps it's patience, focus, or joy. Let these feelings settle into your body, anchoring themselves as part of your experience.

10. (Pause for 1-1.5 minutes.)

11. As you reach the end of this path, take a moment to appreciate the sense of readiness you now feel. Your day is yours to shape, and you are stepping into it with confidence.

12. (Pause for 30 seconds.)

13. Move your fingers and toes, roll your shoulders, and when you're ready, open your eyes. Carry this sense of clarity and purpose with you as you move through your day.

Daily Empowerment Phrases

In line with setting daily intentions, positive phrases can be immensely beneficial. Examples such as "I am capable of achieving my goals" or "I will approach today with gratitude" can be incorporated into morning mindfulness practices to promote motivation and goal-setting. While affirmations provide broad support for mindset shifts, daily empowerment phrases are specifically designed to set the tone for the day ahead. These intentional statements help anchor focus, motivation, and resilience in everyday life.

Encourage your participants to choose phrases that resonate deeply with their personal aspirations and challenges. Suggest that they repeat these phrases aloud or write them down multiple times each morning, integrating them into their breathing exercises or visualization routines. The repetition and belief in these statements can gradually reprogram the subconscious mind, replacing negativity with positivity and hopefulness.

Script #58: Morning Empowerment Meditation

1. Begin by finding a comfortable position, either seated or lying down. Close your eyes and take a slow, deep breath in. Hold for a moment, then exhale fully, letting go of any lingering tension. Feel your body settling into stillness, anchored in this moment.

2. (Pause.)

3. Now, bring to mind a powerful phrase—one that reflects how you want to move through the day ahead. If nothing comes to mind, you may choose from these:

   a. "I am grounded, strong, and ready for today."

   b. "I meet each moment with confidence and clarity.'"

   c. "My actions align with my purpose and strength."

4. Silently repeat your chosen phrase, letting each word resonate within you like a steady drumbeat. With every inhale, invite the energy of these words to fill you. With every exhale, release any self-doubt or hesitation.

5. (Pause for 1-1.5 minutes to repeat the phrase gently with the breath.)

6. Now, imagine this phrase becoming a part of you, flowing through your breath, guiding your thoughts, and shaping your actions. See yourself embodying these words throughout the day—approaching challenges with resilience, speaking with clarity, and embracing moments of joy with a sense of inner strength.

7. (Pause for 1-1.5 minutes.)

8. Take a deep, final inhale, feeling this phrase rooted firmly within you. As you exhale, gently bring awareness back to the present. Wiggle your fingers, stretch if needed, and when you're ready, open your eyes. Step into your day with intention, carrying your chosen words as a quiet source of empowerment.

Integration Tips

To integrate these practices into a seamless morning ritual, suggest breaking them down into manageable segments. For example, those you share these practices with can allocate a few minutes to get comfortable and grounded, followed by a brief session on breath awareness. They can then proceed with visualization for a couple of minutes and close with empowerment phrases to solidify the intention for the day. This structured but flexible routine is adaptable to fit into even the busiest of schedules, ensuring it becomes a sustainable part of your clients' daily lives.

It's also important to emphasize the incremental benefits of these practices. Encourage your clients to remain patient with themselves as they develop this routine. Just like any skill, mastering morning meditations takes time, persistence, and discipline. Remind them that consistency is more important than perfection. Each day offers a new opportunity to refine and deepen their practice, gradually witnessing the cumulative effect on their overall well-being and productivity.

Body Positivity Meditation

Developing a positive connection with oneself and the body can be challenging. An effective way to improve this connection is through appreciation that focuses particularly on your body. This approach can enhance personal self-care and transform how your clients view and treat their bodies. Let's explore some practices that wellness professionals like yoga teachers, life coaches, therapists, and holistic practitioners can utilize to help themselves and their clients nurture a healthier sense of physical appreciation.

Appreciating the Body's Functions

To start, try leading clients in a body scan meditation. This practice involves gently focusing attention on each part of the body, from toes to head, acknowledging and appreciating the function and capability of each area. It's a powerful method that encourages the recognition of the body's resilience and capacity.

Script #59: Body Scan Meditation

1. Sit or lie down in a quiet space where you can fully relax, allowing your body to settle into a comfortable position. Take a slow, deep inhale through your nose, and as you exhale through your mouth, signal your body to relax, letting go of any tension.

2. (Pause.)

3. Now, gently bring your attention to your **forehead**. Notice any tightness or discomfort. As you exhale, imagine that tension dissolving, like a wave of warmth gently softening the muscles. With each breath, feel your forehead smooth and release any strain.

4. (Pause for 30 seconds to allow full attention on the forehead.)

5. Next, move your attention to your **jaw**. Allow yourself to check for any clenching or tightness. With your exhale, imagine the muscles of the jaw releasing, becoming soft and relaxed. Let your mouth slightly part, and feel a sense of ease flowing through this area.

6. (Pause for 30 seconds.)

7. Now, bring your focus to your **neck**. Notice any areas of stiffness or tension. As you breathe out, visualize the tension melting away, leaving your neck free and loose. With each breath, let the muscles soften, creating space between your vertebrae and bringing a gentle sense of release.

8. (Pause for 30 seconds.)

9. Move your attention to your **shoulders**. These are often areas where we hold a lot of stress. As you inhale, notice any tightness or heaviness in your shoulders. With each exhale, imagine that tightness melting away, as if warmth is flowing through your shoulders, allowing them to drop and relax.

10. (Pause for 30 seconds.)

11. Next, bring your awareness to your **arms**. Notice any sensations from the shoulders down to the fingertips. If there is any tension, imagine it gently flowing down your arms, out through your fingertips with each breath. Let the arms feel light and relaxed.

12. (Pause for 30 seconds.)

13. Now, focus on your **chest**. As you breathe, notice how your chest rises and falls. Is there any tightness or discomfort here? With every exhale, imagine a soothing wave of relaxation spreading across your chest, softening any tension, and allowing your heart to feel open and at ease.

14. (Pause for 45 seconds.)

15. Bring your attention to your **abdomen**. Pay attention to how your belly moves with each breath. If there's any tension in this area, imagine it dissolving with your exhale. Picture your abdomen softening with each breath, releasing any tightness, and feeling gentle and calm.

16. (Pause for 45 seconds.)

17. Now, move your focus to your **legs**. Notice any tightness in your thighs, knees, calves, or feet. With each breath, feel the muscles soften and release. Imagine a wave of relaxation traveling down your legs, from your hips to your toes, allowing the entire area to feel light and at ease.

18. (Pause for 30 seconds.)

19. Finally, bring your awareness to your **feet**. Feel the soles of your feet pressing gently into the ground or the surface beneath you. If there's any tension, with every exhale, allow it to melt away. Imagine your feet grounding you, fully relaxed and connected to the earth.

20. (Pause for 30 seconds.)

21. Take a final, deep breath, bringing your awareness back to the present moment. Feel the sense of relaxation that has spread throughout your entire body. When you're ready, gently open your eyes and carry this calm, centered energy with you.

Releasing Negative Body Perceptions

Embracing your body is an important part of growth and emotional well-being. It's common to hold negative perceptions about your body, but those negative perceptions have to be released.

Script #60: Embracing Your Body With Compassion

1. Find a comfortable position, either seated or lying down. Close your eyes gently and take a slow, deep breath in. Hold for a moment, then exhale fully, releasing any tension. Let yourself settle into a space of calm awareness.

2. (Pause for 30 seconds.)

3. Feel appreciation for all your body has carried you through—every step, every movement, every challenge.

4. (Pause for 30 seconds to let the sense of gratitude deepen.)

5. Now, bring your attention to your body. As you breathe, allow these affirmations to resonate within you. Repeat them silently or aloud, letting their meaning sink in.

6. "My body isn't something I should fight because it's a home that protects me." Recognize that your body is not something to fight against but something to nurture and support.

7. (Pause for 45 seconds.)

8. "I release judgment and embrace appreciation." Let go of criticism and allow compassion to take its place. Imagine a sense of warmth filling every part of you.

9. (Pause for 45 seconds.)

10. "I am worthy of care, rest, and love." Acknowledge your body's need for kindness, rest, and nourishment.

11. (Pause for 45 seconds.)

12. "Every day, I grow in appreciation for all that I am." See yourself as a whole being—mind, body, and spirit—worthy of respect and gratitude.

13. (Pause for 45 seconds.)

14. Take a final deep breath in, allowing these affirmations to settle into your consciousness. As you exhale, imagine them becoming a natural part of your thoughts. When you're ready, gently move your fingers and toes, bringing awareness back to the present moment. Open your eyes with a renewed sense of appreciation for yourself. Carry this kindness forward, knowing that your body is your lifelong companion, deserving of care and respect.

Finding Strength in Life's Challenges

Life presents moments of struggle, and challenges can sometimes feel overwhelming. True strength doesn't mean avoiding difficulties; it means developing the ability to navigate them with grace and perseverance.

Meditation can help cultivate this strength by leading to awareness of struggles while helping your clients maintain a sense of calm and stability. Through mindful reflection, breathwork, and affirmations, clients can learn to acknowledge difficulties without resistance, recognizing that struggle is a shared human experience rather than a personal failing.

Encourage participants to view their challenges as moments of growth rather than obstacles. Practicing strength-focused meditation means that they can develop a deeper sense of patience, confidence, and inner steadiness, all of which empower them to move through life with greater ease and self-trust.

Script #61: Struggle Is Part of Being Human

1. Sit comfortably, allowing your hands to rest gently in your lap or over your heart—wherever feels most natural. Close your eyes and take a deep breath in... then exhale slowly, releasing any tension you may be carrying.

2. (Pause.)

3. Now, bring to mind a moment of struggle—something recent, perhaps a difficult interaction, a moment of doubt, or simply a feeling of exhaustion. Hold this experience in your awareness without trying to fix or push it away. Just notice it.

4. (Pause for 45 seconds.)

5. Silently acknowledge to yourself: This is a moment of discomfort. This is a moment of struggle.

6. (Pause for 30 seconds.)

7. Breathe in, allowing space for this truth. There is nothing to fight—only to witness.

8. (Pause for 30 seconds.)

9. Now, remind yourself: "Struggle is part of being human. I am not alone in this." Imagine others—friends, colleagues, even strangers—who may be feeling something similar at this very moment. You are not isolated in your challenges. You are connected to a larger whole.

10. (Pause for 1 minute to allow the feeling of shared humanity to arise.)

11. Now, place a hand gently over your heart or wherever comfort feels most needed. With your next inhale, invite in kindness. Whisper or think to yourself: "May I offer myself the same compassion I would offer a dear friend."

12. (Pause for 30 seconds, letting the words be felt.)

13. Feel the warmth of these words settle into your being. Let them soften the edges of your discomfort.

    a. "May I be patient with myself."

    b. "May I allow myself to rest."

c. "May I acknowledge my needs with love."

14. Breathe deeply, letting these affirmations take root. There is no need to rush. Simply exist in this space of self-compassion.

15. (Pause 1 minute.)

16. When you feel ready, take a final deep inhale. As you exhale, visualize tension leaving your body, replaced with a sense of ease. Gently move your fingers and toes, returning to the present moment with the knowledge that you can return to this practice whenever you need.

The Power of Self-Trust

In a time that often measures worth by achievement and productivity, it's easy to lose sight of an important truth: Your value is not something to be earned—it is something inherent. Self-trust is the basis of embracing one's worth, allowing us to stand firm in who we are without seeking validation from external sources. Meditation can be a great way to strengthen self-trust. Reflecting on personal experiences, recognizing inner strengths, and affirming one's value through meditation can help those you work with deepen their confidence in their own decisions and abilities.

Script #62: Rooted in Self-Trust Meditation

1. Let your hands rest naturally—on your lap or over your heart. Close your eyes and take a steady breath in... hold it briefly... then exhale slowly, releasing any tension.

2. (Pause.)

3. As you settle into your breath, picture yourself at a younger age—a version of you at five or six years old. Notice the curiosity in your eyes and the openness in your expression. This was you before life added layers of expectations and self-doubt.

4. (Pause for 30 seconds, letting this image form.)

5. Now, imagine standing before this younger version of yourself. Look at them—really see them—and acknowledge their hopes and their fears. Gently, in your mind, say: You are enough, just as you are.

6. (Pause for 30 seconds.)

7. Breathe deeply, allowing these words to sink in.

8. (Allow 30 seconds of reflective breathing.)

9. Shift your focus to the present, picturing yourself as you are today. Reflect on everything you've navigated—the struggles, the wins, the moments of growth. Without judgment, see yourself fully and honestly. Remind yourself: "I am still enough. I don't need to prove my worth."

10. (Pause for 30 seconds.)

11. With each breath, imagine a quiet sense of self-trust building within you—steady, calm, and real. Trust that you have the wisdom and strength to navigate life's challenges.

12. (Pause for 45 seconds.)

13. Silently repeat:

    a. "I am allowed to be a work in progress."

    b. "I don't need to be perfect to have worth and value."

    c. "I trust myself to make choices that align with what's truly best for me."

14. Let these words settle into your mind. They are not just phrases—they are truths.

15. (Pause for 30 seconds.)

16. When you're ready, take a final, steady breath in, anchoring this sense of self-compassion. As you exhale, move your fingers and toes slightly, bringing awareness back to your surroundings. Open your eyes when you're ready, carrying this calm assurance with you into the rest of your day.

17. (Pause briefly before closing.)

18. You are enough—always.

Digital Detox Meditation

In recent years, screens have become an unavoidable part of daily life. From work emails to social media notifications, the constant stream of digital input can be overwhelming and mentally exhausting. A digital detox meditation practice will help your clients regain a sense of balance by creating awareness, grounding the mind, and encouraging mindful breaks from technology. The following meditations are designed to help participants reduce screen fatigue and cultivate a healthier relationship with digital devices.

Awareness of Screen Overload

The first step in reducing digital overwhelm is recognizing its impact. Many people experience symptoms of screen overload without realizing it—eye strain, restlessness, mental fog, and increased stress. Encouraging participants to acknowledge these signs helps them become more mindful of their screen usage and make intentional choices about their digital consumption. The following meditation helps cultivate awareness of digital fatigue while leading to a sense of clarity and control.

Script #63: Reclaiming Your Attention

1. Sit comfortably, letting your hands rest naturally. Take a slow, steady breath in... and a long, releasing breath out. Gently close your eyes and allow your body to settle.

2. (Pause for 30 seconds to let the body relax.)

3. Now, think about your day—how often you've picked up your phone, checked a screen, or shifted from one digital task to another. There's no need to judge these moments—just notice them, like an observer watching from a distance.

4. (Allow 45 seconds to reflect.)

5. Shift your awareness to how your body feels. Are your shoulders tight? Your jaw clenched? Your mind racing from one thought to the next? Simply acknowledge these sensations.

6. (Pause for 30 seconds to let participants observe bodily tensions.)

7. With each inhale, picture yourself reclaiming a sense of calm. With each exhale, let go of the mental noise, the endless notifications, the pull of distraction.

8. (Allow 1 minute of slow breathing.)

9. Now, ask yourself: "When was the last time I was fully present—without a screen?" What did that moment feel like? Let that feeling rise within you—a sense of clarity, stillness, or connection.

10. (Pause for 30-45 seconds.)

11. Breathe deeply, allowing this grounded presence to settle in. Remind yourself that your attention is yours to guide. You can choose moments of stillness, just as you are doing now.

12. (Pause.)

13. When you're ready, take a final, centering breath. Gently move your fingers and toes, and open your eyes. Move forward with the quiet knowledge that your attention is a powerful tool—one you can reclaim, again and again.

Reconnecting With Your Senses

When we spend too much time on screens, our senses can feel dulled—like we're living through a filter. This practice is about reawakening those senses, giving your mind a break from the digital world.

Script #64: Reconnecting With Your Senses

1. Find a quiet space and take a deep breath in, letting the air expand your lungs... then slowly release it.

2. (Pause.)

3. Start by noticing the physical world around you. Feel the surface beneath you—whether it's the chair supporting your weight or the floor pressing against your feet. Run your fingers lightly over your clothing or a nearby object, paying attention to its temperature and texture.

4. (Pause for 30-45 seconds.)

5. Now, turn your focus to sound. Without searching for noise, simply notice what's there—the subtle hum of a distant appliance, a breeze outside, or the soft rhythm of your own breath. Let the sounds come and go.

6. (Pause 1 minute.)

7. If there's a scent in the air, breathe it in naturally. It might be faint or familiar—perhaps the smell of your surroundings or something subtle you hadn't noticed until now.

8. (Pause for 30-45 seconds.)

9. Gently open your eyes and take in your surroundings. Instead of looking at screens, observe small details—the way light falls on a surface, the variety of shapes and colors around you. Let yourself notice without rushing.

10. (Allow 30-45 seconds for participants to visually explore their space.)

11. Finally, return to your breath. Inhale deeply and exhale fully. Remind yourself that your senses are always with you—an anchor to the present moment, beyond the pull of screens.

Script #65: Mental Reset Meditation

1. Sit comfortably, placing your hands on your lap or over your heart. Close your eyes and begin by gently focusing on the rhythm of your thoughts. Acknowledge that your mind has been active and influenced by digital inputs. There's no need to judge this; simply notice it.

2. (Pause for 1 minute.)

3. Now, let's introduce a pause. Without trying to control anything, let the space between your thoughts gradually grow longer. Allow your mind to simply exist, without engaging in any judgments or new inputs. If your thoughts start to race, gently remind yourself that you don't need to respond to them right now.

4. (Pause for 1-2 minutes.)

5. Instead of focusing on your breath, body, or images, turn your attention to the subtle shifts in your awareness. You're not trying to force relaxation or stillness—just allowing the natural process of mental quiet to emerge. Let your mind have a break from stimulation, even if just for a few moments.

6. (Pause for 2-3 minutes, with brief reminders to stay with the stillness.)

7. When you feel the mental noise has softened, gently open your eyes. Notice how your thoughts have settled into a more neutral and balanced state. You're now prepared to continue your day with clarity and a refreshed sense of focus.

Navigating Social Media's Mental Load

Social media can be a double-edged sword, as it can both connect us and cloud our minds with comparison, information overload, and the pressure to stay visible. Taking intentional pauses from these platforms is vital for protecting mental clarity and emotional balance.

Script #66: Releasing Approval Dependency and Owning Your Worth

1. Find a comfortable position, whether seated or lying down, and allow your body to relax fully. Rest your hands gently in your lap or by your sides. Close your eyes if it feels right and take a deep, calming breath in... and slowly release it, letting go of any tension.

2. (Pause.)

3. Take a moment to reflect on how you might feel the pull of comparison, envy, or the need for external approval. Notice any moments when you measure your success or your worth by others' achievements or opinions. Acknowledge these feelings with kindness, knowing they are a natural part of being human, but they do not define who you are.

4. (Pause for 1-2 minutes for reflection.)

5. In this space, remind yourself:

a. "My worth is not determined by the opinions or successes of others."

b. "I am enough as I am, and I don't need to compare myself to anyone."

c. "I release the need for validation, trusting in my own value."

6. (Pause for 30 seconds.)

7. Take a moment now to think about what truly matters to you in your life. What brings you joy, fulfillment, and peace? These are the things that truly define your worth. Reconnect with these qualities now.

8. (Pause for 1-2 minutes.)

9. As you breathe, repeat the following affirmations softly to yourself:

a. "I am worthy of love and respect, simply because I am me."

b. "My path is unique, and I trust it to unfold at its own pace."

c. "I choose to honor my journey, free from comparison and the need for approval."

10. Feel these words deeply, like seeds of self-compassion taking root in your heart. Let them gently replace any thoughts or feelings that have made you doubt your own value.

11. (Pause for 30-45 seconds.)

12. Now, take a moment to imagine yourself fully embracing who you are, exactly as you are—without the need for comparison, validation, or external measures of success. Picture yourself walking through life with a sense of peace, confidence, and deep trust in your own path.

13. (Pause 1 minute.)

14. When you feel ready, gently open your eyes, bringing this newfound sense of self-worth with you.

15. Remember: your value is not based on anyone else's journey or opinions. You are whole, worthy, and powerful, just as you are.

Bringing It All Together

In this chapter, we talked about the importance of helping participants start their day with a clear mind and strong intentions through meditation. It's all geared toward creating a calming space for your clients, so that they can also carry into their daily life even outside of sessions with you. These morning rituals aren't quick fixes, but they are effective tools for building mental and emotional resilience over time.

Chapter 8:

Integrating Mindfulness and Meditation Into Diverse Practices

Meditation and mindfulness aren't confined to quiet therapy rooms—they can seamlessly integrate into various practices, enriching the well-being of those you work with. Be it through movement, sound, or energy work, mindfulness adapts to diverse needs, promoting clarity, peace, and connection. This chapter explores creative ways to incorporate mindfulness into your practice in order to help clients experience its incredible effects in ways that resonate with them.

Mindful Movement

Mindful movement involves engaging your body in gentle, intentional movement while maintaining present-moment awareness. Unlike Movement Integration in Chapter 3, which focuses on synchronizing small movements with breath, mindful movement extends beyond breathwork into full-body practices that promote embodiment, energy flow, and mental clarity.

Rather than emphasizing performance or physical outcomes, mindful movement is about deepening the connection between body, breath, and mind. It encourages participants to listen to their bodies, honor their limitations, and move with awareness. Common forms of mindful movement include:

- **Yoga:** A practice combining breath, postures, and meditation to cultivate awareness.

- **Tai Chi:** A slow, flowing martial art that enhances energy flow and mental clarity.

- **Qigong:** Gentle movements designed to cultivate life force energy and promote healing.

- **Walking Meditation:** Moving with full awareness of each step, focusing on the feet's connection to the earth.

- **Somatic Movement:** Free-form, intuitive movements that emphasize sensation, releasing tension stored in the body.

The Benefits of Mindful Movement

Mindful movement offers a wide range of physical, emotional, and mental benefits:

- **Reduces Stress and Anxiety:** Gentle movement paired with breath awareness calms the nervous system.

- **Improves Body Awareness:** Tuning into physical sensations helps recognize tension or imbalance.

- **Enhances Focus and Concentration:** Intentional movement creates a meditative state for mental clarity.

- **Supports Emotional Regulation:** Movement releases stored emotions and promotes emotional resilience.

- **Increases Flexibility and Strength:** Many practices improve mobility, balance, and strength over time.

Script #67: Embodied Awareness

This script takes a somatic approach to mindful movement, guiding awareness through subtle shifts in posture and sensation.

1. Begin by finding a comfortable seated or standing position. Let your body settle naturally, feeling the surface beneath you supporting your weight. If it feels right, close your eyes or soften your gaze, allowing your attention to shift inward.

2. (Pause for 30 seconds.)

3. Start by bringing awareness to your breath—not changing it, just noticing. Feel the air entering through your nostrils, the subtle rise and fall of your chest. With each exhale, imagine tension melting away like a gentle wave receding from the shore.

4. (Allow 1 minute for slow, conscious breaths.)

5. Now, shift your focus to your sense of touch. Notice how warm or cool the space around you feels on your skin. Feel the texture of your clothing, the weight of your hands resting on your lap or by your sides. If standing, sense the ground beneath your feet—its firmness, its stability.

6. (Pause 1 minute.)

7. Next, bring attention to sound. Allow your ears to take in the noises around you, whether distant or close. Notice the rhythm of your breath joining this soundscape. There is no need to judge—simply observe, letting each sound come and go.

8. (Pause 1 minute.)

9. Now, gently turn your awareness to movement. Begin with the smallest motion—a slight tilt of your head, the soft flex of your fingers. Roll your shoulders gently, noticing the sensation of muscles awakening. If standing, shift your weight slightly from one foot to the other, tuning in to how your body naturally seeks balance.

10. (Pause 1 minute.)

11. As you continue, imagine energy flowing through you, a quiet hum of life within. Feel the presence of your body—not as a

collection of thoughts or judgments, but as a living, breathing experience.

12. (Pause 1 minute.)

13. Finish the meditation with another deep inhale, taking note of the sensation of the air filling your lungs. As you exhale, release any remaining tension, carrying this sense of embodied presence into the rest of your day.

Sound Healing and Mindfulness

Another technique you can integrate is sound healing. Sound healing is an ancient practice that uses different vibrational frequencies to elevate relaxation, balance energy, and support emotional and physical healing. Various cultures have harnessed the power of sound for centuries, as they have recognized its ability to influence the mind and body. The human body is highly responsive to sound, as different frequencies can alter brainwave activity, reduce stress, and enhance meditative states (Paszkiel et al., 2020). When integrated with mindfulness, sound healing becomes a powerful way to deepen awareness and facilitate inner harmony.

There are many methods of sound healing that you can incorporate into different meditations, each with unique benefits:

- **Singing Bowls (Tibetan and Crystal):** These bowls produce resonant tones that promote deep relaxation and energetic alignment.

- **Tuning Fork Therapy:** Specific frequencies from tuning forks are applied to the body or energy field to restore balance.

- **Binaural Beats:** Two slightly different frequencies are played in each ear, creating a perceived third tone that influences brainwave activity.

- **Chanting and Mantras:** Repeating sacred sounds, words, or phrases to focus the mind and raise vibrational energy.

- **Gongs and Drumming:** Rhythmic and harmonic sounds that help clear energetic blockages and induce meditative states.

- **Nature Sounds:** The soothing sounds of water, wind, or birds can create a calming and grounding effect.

Benefits of Integrating Sound With Mindfulness

Combining sound healing with mindfulness enhances the meditative experience, offering:

- **Deepened Relaxation:** The resonance of sound can guide the mind into a state of profound stillness.

- **Emotional Release:** Certain frequencies help release stored emotions and trauma.

- **Heightened Awareness:** Sound can serve as an anchor for present-moment focus.

- **Enhanced Energy Flow:** Vibrational frequencies help unblock stagnant energy in the body.

- **Improved Sleep and Stress Reduction:** Sound healing reduces cortisol levels and promotes restorative sleep.

Let's take a moment now to explore some different sound-based meditation scripts that you can introduce to those you work with.

Script #68: The Resonance of Sound

You can work with this script to help you integrate sound into group meditation sessions you host.

1. (Invite participants to sit comfortably, ensuring they are relaxed but alert. Once the group is settled, begin.)

2. Close your eyes and take a moment to arrive in this space. Notice the air around you, the way your body rests in its seat. Now, shift your awareness to the sounds within this room—the faint rustling of clothing, the gentle hum of presence. Let these sounds settle into the background, neither grasping at them nor pushing them away.

3. (Allow 45 seconds for participants to observe the sounds.)

4. In a moment, you will hear the first sound—a single tone resonating in the space. When you hear it, simply listen. Let it move through you, without expectation or effort.

5. (Strike a Tibetan singing bowl or another resonant instrument, allowing the sound to fade naturally.)

6. As the sound dissolves, notice its echo—not just in the air, but in your own awareness. How does the silence feel in its absence? Does a subtle vibration linger within you?

7. (Pause until the sound fades completely.)

8. Now, together, we will bring our breath into harmony with sound. With the next tone, inhale slowly, following the rise of the sound. Hold for a moment at the peak. Then, as the sound fades, exhale with it, releasing fully.

9. (Play the sound again, guiding the group through synchronized breathing.)

10. Inhale as the sound swells… hold… and exhale as it fades.

11. (Repeat for several cycles, gradually allowing the group to internalize the rhythm.)

12. As the sound settles into silence, let your breath continue in this natural rhythm. Notice the stillness it leaves behind, the

way the energy in the room has shifted. Even without sound, a quiet resonance remains, a shared frequency among us all.

13. (Allow another minute for participants to rest in this space before gently guiding them back.)

14. Now, slowly bring awareness back to your body, to the weight of your presence here. When you feel ready, open your eyes, carrying this quiet resonance with you.

Script #69: Sound Meditation for Deep Focus and Relaxation

This meditation uses sound as an anchor for awareness, allowing the mind to settle and the body to relax. It is suitable for both seated and reclined positions and can be integrated into a yoga practice.

1. Find a comfortable seated or reclined position, allowing your body to settle into stillness. Let your eyes close or focus on something softly as you deepen your inner awareness.

2. (Pause for 30 seconds.)

3. Begin by tuning in to the sounds around you—the distant hum of the world, the subtle rustling of breath, the resonance of the space you are in. There is no need to judge or label these sounds; simply observe them as they come and go.

4. (Pause for 45 seconds to let awareness settle on ambient sound.)

5. Now, as you begin to settle into the soundscape around you, I will introduce a tone to guide our shared awareness.

6. (Ring a singing bowl, chime, or softly play a resonant instrument.)

7. Allow the sound to reach you fully. Feel its vibration, as if the sound is not just something you hear but something you experience with your whole body.

8. (Pause until the sound fades.)

9. With each strike of the sound, follow its fading resonance until it dissolves into silence. Notice the space between sounds, the quiet moments where stillness emerges.

10. If thoughts arise, acknowledge them and let them drift away, like ripples expanding and softening in water. Each sound guides you deeper into a state of focus and ease.

11. (Continue playing soft tones at intervals, allowing time for deep listening.)

12. Now, bring your attention to your breath, noticing how it moves in harmony with the sounds. Each inhale invites clarity; each exhale releases tension.

13. (Pause 1 minute for breath awareness.)

14. As we prepare to close, allow the final sound to linger in your awareness, a gentle reminder of presence and peace.

15. (Final chime or tone.)

16. When you are ready, take a deep breath in… and exhale slowly. In your own time, open your eyes, carrying this sense of stillness with you into the rest of your day.

Script #70: Mantra Meditation for Inner Peace

1. Find a comfortable seated position, ensuring your spine is tall yet relaxed. Gently close your eyes and take a deep breath in… and a slow, steady exhale out. Feel your body settle into stillness.

2. (Pause for a few breaths.)

3. Now, bring your awareness to your breath, allowing it to flow naturally. With your next inhale, begin to chant a simple mantra—perhaps "Om," the universal sound of connection, or

"So Hum," meaning "I am that." Choose a mantra that resonates with you, either spoken aloud or repeated silently in your mind.

4. (Allow 30-45 seconds to let them settle into the mantra.)

5. As you chant, feel the vibration of the sound resonating in your chest, your throat, and even beyond your body. Let the mantra synchronize with your breath—inhale, then chant on the exhale. Allow each repetition to draw you deeper into stillness, like waves gently lapping at the shore.

6. (Pause for 1 minute of mantra repetition.)

7. If your mind begins to wander, acknowledge the distraction without judgment, then gently return to the rhythm of your mantra. Each repetition is a thread, weaving a bridge between your inner and outer world, between breath and awareness.

8. (Pause again for 1-2 minutes.)

9. Continue for several minutes, allowing the sound to become effortless, as if it is chanting itself through you. Feel how the mantra creates space within you—clearing, centering, soothing.

10. (Pause another 2-3 minutes.)

11. When you feel ready, let the mantra dissolve into silence, but remain present with the subtle energy it has created. Sit in this quiet stillness, absorbing the sense of peace you have cultivated.

12. (Pause for 30-45 seconds.)

13. Take one more deep breath in… and release the air from your lungs slowly. When you are ready, open your eyes, carrying this inner harmony with you into the rest of your day.

Chakra Balancing Meditations

Chakras are energy centers within the body that influence physical, emotional, and spiritual well-being. The chakra system—rooted in ancient Hindu traditions—was later incorporated into certain Buddhist practices, particularly in Tibetan and Tantric Buddhism. While the concept of energy centers exists in both traditions, their interpretations and structures may differ. The system most commonly recognized today consists of seven primary chakras, each associated with specific aspects of life and consciousness. When these energy centers are balanced, people experience harmony and vitality. However, blockages or imbalances can lead to emotional distress, physical discomfort, or spiritual disconnection.

The seven main chakras include:

1. **Root Chakra (Muladhara)**: grounding, stability, security

2. **Sacral Chakra (Svadhisthana)**: creativity, emotions, sensuality

3. **Solar Plexus Chakra (Manipura)**: confidence, personal power, motivation

4. **Heart Chakra (Anahata)**: love, compassion, connection

5. **Throat Chakra (Vishuddha)**: communication, truth, self-expression

6. **Third Eye Chakra (Ajna)**: intuition, insight, wisdom

7. **Crown Chakra (Sahasrara)**: spiritual connection, enlightenment

There are various techniques to balance the chakras and restore energetic flow. For example, meditation can be a great technique. Guided visualizations and breathwork can help activate and harmonize each chakra. Beyond that, sound, colors, crystals, aromatherapy, and even yoga can be integrated into chakra healing practices to create balance and stability in different areas of life.

Script #71: Full Chakra Alignment Meditation

1. Find a comfortable seated or lying position. Close your eyes and take a deep breath in, exhaling fully. Imagine a warm, grounding energy at the base of your spine, glowing a deep red. With each inhale, feel this energy strengthening your sense of security. As you exhale, release any fear or tension.

2. (Pause for 30-45 seconds.)

3. Move your awareness up to your lower abdomen, visualizing a bright orange light. This is your sacral chakra—breathe into it, welcoming creativity and emotional balance.

4. (Pause for 30 seconds.)

5. Shift your focus to your solar plexus, just above your navel. Picture a golden yellow light, radiating confidence and personal power. With each breath, feel your inner strength growing.

6. (Pause for 30-45 seconds.)

7. Now, bring your attention to your heart center, glowing green. Allow feelings of love and compassion to expand, filling your entire body with warmth.

8. (Pause for 45 seconds to let them rest in the heart space.)

9. As you inhale, direct your awareness to your throat, seeing a clear blue light. Feel your voice, truth, and expression becoming more fluid and confident.

10. (Pause for 30-45 seconds.)

11. Gently move up to the space between your eyebrows, your third eye chakra. A deep indigo light emerges, opening the door to intuition and insight.

12. (Pause for 30-45 seconds.)

13. Finally, bring your awareness to the crown of your head, where a radiant violet or white light shines. Feel your connection to the universe expanding, filling you with wisdom and peace.

14. (Pause for 45-60 seconds.)

15. Take a few more deep breaths, allowing all chakras to align in harmony. When you're ready, return your focus to the present moment and slowly open your eyes.

Script #72: Heart Chakra Opening Meditation

1. Sit comfortably and place your hands over your heart, feeling the gentle rhythm beneath your palms.

2. (Pause for 30 seconds.)

3. Close your eyes and take a slow, deep breath in. Imagine a soft green light swirling at the center of your chest—the heart chakra. With each inhale, this light expands, filling your chest with warmth and compassion. With each exhale, release any tension or heaviness, allowing it to dissolve like mist.

4. (Pause for 30-45 seconds.)

5. Now, bring to mind someone you wish to send love to—a friend, a family member, or even yourself. Picture them standing before you, their heart glowing softly. Visualize the green light from your heart flowing to theirs—a steady stream of unconditional love. See their heart respond, the two lights blending, forming a quiet bridge of connection.

6. (Pause for 45 seconds.)

7. Let this energy ripple outwards, extending beyond both of you, touching others, and radiating into the world.

8. (Pause for 30-45 seconds.)

9. After a few moments, gently draw the green light back into your heart, where it settles like a glowing ember—steady, warm, and constant.

10. (Pause for 30 seconds.)

11. Take a final deep breath. Wiggle your fingers and toes, then softly open your eyes, carrying this feeling of love with you into the rest of your day.

Script #73: Root Chakra Grounding Meditation

1. Stand or sit with your feet firmly planted on the ground, your spine straight, and your shoulders relaxed.

2. (Pause.)

3. Let your eyes fall closed and take a strong but gentle breath. Visualize strong, deep roots extending from the soles of your feet, pushing down into the earth, anchoring you in place.

4. (Pause for 30-45 seconds.)

5. With each inhale, draw in the solid, steady energy of the ground beneath you—a quiet strength rising through your legs, into your core, and along your spine.

6. (Pause for 30-45 seconds.)

7. As you exhale, release any tension, doubt, or restlessness. Let them sink down through the roots, absorbed by the earth.

8. (Pause for 30-45 seconds.)

9. Keep this rhythm—breathing in stability, breathing out anything weighing you down. Feel yourself becoming more centered, more grounded, rooted in both mind and body.

10. (Pause for 1-1.5 minutes, allowing space to deepen into this rhythm.)

11. After another moment, take another deep inhale as you bring yourself back to the present. Open your eyes and move forward with a steady sense of focus and control.

Script #74: Throat Chakra Expression Meditation

1. Find a comfortable seated position, allowing your spine to lengthen and your shoulders to relax. Gently close your eyes and take a deep breath in through your nose, then exhale slowly.

2. (Pause.)

3. Bring your awareness to your throat, the center of communication and self-expression. Notice any tension or tightness there, and as you breathe, allow it to soften. With each inhale, invite a sense of openness; with each exhale, release any hesitation or fear of speaking your truth.

4. (Pause for 30-45 seconds.)

5. Now, silently repeat the affirmation: "My voice is clear, my words are true, and I express myself with confidence and ease."

6. (Pause for 30-45 seconds.)

7. Feel the gentle movement of your breath in your throat, the space where thoughts become words. If there is something you've been holding back, imagine speaking it freely, feeling the ease of authentic expression.

8. (Pause for 45-60 seconds.)

9. Continue to breathe steadily, embracing a sense of confidence in your voice. When you're ready, take a final deep breath, gently open your eyes, and move forward with a feeling of clarity and self-assurance.

Ayurvedic Approaches to Meditation

You can also work with Ayurvedic principles alongside mindfulness and meditation to help your clients experience a more holistic level of healing. Ayurveda, the ancient Indian system of holistic healing, is based on the principle that well-being arises from a balance between mind, body, and spirit. Ayurveda incorporates the three doshas—Vata, Pitta, and Kapha—which represent different energies and govern physiological and psychological functions. Meditation practices rooted in Ayurveda align with an individual's dominant dosha, helping restore balance and promote overall health.

Vata is associated with air and ether, and governs movement, creativity, and flexibility. When imbalanced, it can cause anxiety, restlessness, and scattered thoughts. Pitta—linked to fire and water—rules digestion, intellect, and transformation. An excess of Pitta can lead to anger, frustration, and burnout. Kapha, connected to earth and water, controls stability, structure, and nourishment. An imbalance in Kapha can manifest as lethargy, resistance to change, or emotional heaviness. Understanding one's dosha means that meditation techniques can be tailored to support individual needs, which is an important consideration to bear in mind while sharing meditation techniques with others.

With this in mind, based on the needs of your client, you can use different meditation scripts to harness the power of Ayurvedic meditation and show your participants the incredible benefits it stands to offer them.

Script #75: Grounding Vata Meditation

1. Sit comfortably, either on the floor or in a chair, ensuring that your feet are firmly planted on the ground. Bring your eyes to a gentle close and softly inhale. Let the breath fill your lungs, and exhale fully, releasing any tension in your body.

2. (Pause.)

3. Bring awareness to your body, noting how it feels in the space you're in. Vata energy is often light and expansive, so ground yourself by becoming aware of the earth beneath you, offering a steady base. Feel your feet connecting with the ground beneath, anchoring you in the present moment.

4. (Pause for 30-45 seconds.)

5. With each inhale, imagine the earth beneath your feet providing a solid foundation, drawing stability into your body. As you exhale, let go of any feelings of instability or restlessness, allowing your mind to quiet and your body to settle into the space.

6. (Allow 1 minute for visualization and rhythmic breathing.)

7. Take a moment to feel the weight of your body, letting the solid, grounding force of the earth balance the lightness of Vata energy.

8. (Pause for 45 seconds.)

9. Mentally repeat a grounding mantra, such as "I am rooted, I am present," until you feel calm, stable, and steady. Allow the rhythm of your breath to help bring balance to any scattered or erratic thoughts.

10. (Allow 1.5-2 minutes for participants to mentally repeat the mantra.)

11. When you're ready, gently open your eyes, carrying this sense of grounded presence into your day.

Script #76: Cooling Pitta Meditation

1. Find a cool, peaceful space to sit comfortably. Close your eyes and take a deep breath in, allowing your belly to expand gently. Exhale slowly, releasing any heat or tension in your body, letting go of anything that's built up.

2. (Pause for a few breaths, letting the body settle.)

3. Picture a calm, clear lake—its surface smooth, reflecting the moonlight. Now, imagine stepping into the cool water, feeling it rise around your ankles, then your legs, bringing relief to any lingering heat. As you move deeper, the water embraces you, its gentle touch soothing your body and mind.

4. (Pause to let the imagery fully form.)

5. With each inhale, draw in the lake's cooling energy, letting it settle in your chest, your heart, your mind, washing away any intensity or restlessness. With each exhale, release frustration, irritation, or tension, allowing the water to carry it away.

6. (Pause for 45-60 seconds to breath with the visualization.)

7. Feel yourself floating effortlessly, weightless and at ease. Silently repeat the mantra "I am calm, I am at peace," letting the words reinforce this cooling, tranquil state.

8. (Pause for 1-2 minutes.)

9. When you're ready, take a final deep breath and slowly step out of the water in your mind's eye. Open your eyes, carrying this deep sense of calm with you throughout your day.

Script #77: Energizing Kapha Meditation

1. Sit upright with a strong, alert posture, feeling a sense of readiness in your body. Take a deep breath in, lifting your chest, and exhale with purpose, releasing any sluggishness or fatigue.

2. (Pause for a few breaths.)

3. Begin a rhythmic breathing pattern: inhale deeply for four counts, hold briefly, and exhale in three or four short, forceful bursts. Let each breath grow more powerful, as if you're

energizing your entire body with the inhale and expelling heaviness with each exhale.

4. (Allow 1-2 minutes for participants to continue this breath cycle.)

5. Now, visualize a steady flow of energy moving from the center of your chest outward, like a bright sun rising with power and purpose. Feel this energy waking up your body, bringing strength and vitality to every part of you.

6. (Pause for 30-45 seconds to let the imagery build.)

7. Repeat silently or aloud the mantra "I am energized, I am motivated," letting each breath charge you with a sense of drive and purpose. Feel your body growing more alert and invigorated with every inhale.

8. (Pause for 1-2 minutes.)

9. When you're ready, open your eyes, feeling focused, energized, and prepared to take on the day.

Combining different practices alongside meditation has the potential to deepen the experience for your clients, which can make meditation far more meaningful and supportive when it comes to their individual needs. You can tap into time-tested wisdom and techniques to improve your practice and your clients' wellness by incorporating different techniques.

Chapter 9:

Scripts for Teaching Groups and Classes

Teaching meditation to groups and classes is an exciting way to improve individual practices through shared experiences. In these sessions, participants can connect on a deeper level by exploring mindfulness together in a way that enhances both personal growth and group dynamics. Guided meditations tailored for these settings offer unique opportunities to explore different aspects of mindfulness, thus creating a supportive environment where everyone can learn and grow. You can modify each one as needed to better suit your group, of course.

Engaging Group Meditations

Creating connection and participation in group settings with engaging meditation scripts can turn the meditation experience from a solitary practice into a communal experience. By using various methods like dynamic group energy meditations, themed group meditations, guided visualizations, and interactive group reflections, you can create unique and impactful experiences that leave lasting impressions on participants.

Dynamic Group Energy Meditations

Dynamic group energy meditations are particularly powerful in group settings. They leverage collective intention to amplify individual benefits. When participants gather with a common purpose or goal, the energy within the group is elevated, which creates a more impactful meditation experience for everyone involved. Synchronizing practices—such as breathing in unison or focusing on shared mantras—can further enhance this energy.

Script #78: Dynamic Group Energy Meditation

In group meditation, the energy of collective intention can amplify individual experiences, creating a powerful sense of connection. This meditation is designed to harness that energy through synchronized breathing, visualization, and shared focus to build a unified yet dynamic presence. Consciously breathing and setting intentions together means that participants will feel a tangible exchange of energy, strengthening both personal and communal awareness.

1. (Begin by inviting everyone to sit in a comfortable position, ensuring that each person has enough space while still feeling connected to the group. Encourage participants to rest their hands on their knees or place their palms upward in an open, receptive posture.)

2. Close your eyes and take a deep breath in through your nose. Feel the air filling your lungs, expanding your ribs, and nourishing your body. Hold this breath for a brief moment, sensing the shared stillness around you. Now, exhale together, releasing any tension, any distractions, letting the breath flow out as one.

3. (Pause, allowing a few rounds of natural breathing.)

4. As we breathe together, notice the subtle rhythm forming in the space. The sound of the inhales, the gentle exhalations, the presence of those beside you. Feel the collective energy in this room—each breath, each heartbeat adding to the shared current of intention.

5. (Pause, then guide the group into a slow, rhythmic breathing pattern.)

6. Inhale for four counts… 1, 2, 3, 4… Hold… 2, 3… Exhale… 1, 2, 3, 4… Hold… 2, 3… Let's continue this cycle, moving as one, creating a steady, flowing breath together.

7. (After a several cycles, transition into visualization.)

8. Now, bring your awareness to the space between you and the others in this group. Imagine the energy of your breath weaving through this space like an invisible thread, connecting each person to the whole. With every inhale, draw in a sense of unity, of belonging. With every exhale, release any feeling of separateness, allowing yourself to merge into this shared presence.

9. (Let the group sit in this awareness for 30-45 seconds, breathing together.)

10. As we continue, bring to mind a single word that represents the intention of this group. Perhaps it is peace, strength, clarity, or love. Whatever arises naturally, hold it in your mind. On your next inhale, silently invite this energy into your body. On your exhale, send it outward, offering it to the space and those around you.

11. (Allow 1-2 minutes of silent mantra repetition before bringing the meditation to a close.)

12. Now, return to your natural breath. Notice how the air moves through you effortlessly, how the energy of this space has shifted. When you are ready, gently stretch your fingers, roll your shoulders, and open your eyes, knowing that the collective energy we have created lingers within you, supporting you even as you move beyond this moment.

13. (Encourage the group to acknowledge each other before transitioning back to normal activity, reinforcing the sense of shared experience.)

Script #79: Collective Stillness Meditation

Stillness has a profound way of connecting people, even without words or movement. This meditation focuses on subtle awareness—the quiet presence of others, the shared space, and the unspoken connection that naturally forms when a group sits in stillness. Rather than synchronizing breath or energy, this practice encourages participants to simply notice—to tune into the gentle unity that exists when people gather in mindful silence.

1. (Invite the group to find a comfortable seated position, ensuring everyone feels at ease yet aware of the shared space around them.)

2. Relax your eyes and let yourself find a sense of peace. Feel the ground beneath you, steady and solid, supporting your weight. Stretch your spine upwards so you're sitting up straight, let your shoulders drop and relax, and have your hands rest gently in your lap.

3. (Pause for a few natural breaths.)

4. Begin by tuning into your own breath. Notice the gentle rise and fall of your chest, the quiet rhythm that moves through you without effort or force. Each inhale... each exhale... a steady, familiar pattern.

5. (Let the group sit with their breath for 30-45 seconds.)

6. Now, widen your awareness. Sense the presence of the others in this space—not through sight, but through feeling. The quiet inhales and exhales happening all around you. Each person breathing at their own pace, yet sharing the same air, the same moment.

7. (Pause for 30 seconds to introduce a sense of subtle unity.)

8. Without needing to change your breath, notice how the space seems to shift—how the silence between us holds a quiet

connection. Though we sit as individuals, we are part of something shared.

9. (Allow the group to settle into this awareness for 45-60 seconds.)

10. Now, bring to mind a simple word or feeling that reflects what you'd like this group to hold—perhaps calm, presence, or support. Let this word settle within you, without needing to force it.

11. (Pause.)

12. With your next inhale, quietly welcome this feeling into your body. With your exhale, release it into the room, offering it to the shared space between us.

13. (Guide the group for 1-2 minutes of this soft, intentional breathing.)

14. As we begin to close, let your awareness return fully to yourself. Feel your own breath... your own presence... while still holding the quiet knowledge that this group energy remains.

15. (Pause for 30 seconds.)

16. Take a few deeper breaths at your own pace. Wiggle your fingers, roll your shoulders, and when you're ready, slowly open your eyes—carrying this sense of quiet connection with you.

Themed Group Meditations

Themed group meditations incorporate another layer of engagement by centering sessions around specific topics or themes. Directing the focus toward a shared subject means that you can encourage reflection and discussion among participants while simultaneously building a group bond. The following scripts are examples of different themes you can incorporate into group sessions to amplify the benefits of meditation in support of a group-focused goal or need.

Script #80: The Thread of Gratitude

1. (Invite the group to sit comfortably, allowing them to settle into a space where they feel both supported and connected to those around them. Encourage an upright yet relaxed posture, hands resting naturally.)

2. Rest your eyes and let your mind focus on the rhythm of your breathing. No need to change it—just observe. The way it moves in, the way it moves out. The way it connects you to this moment, and to the people sharing this space with you.

3. (Pause for 30 seconds to allow the group to settle.)

4. Today, we gather with a shared intention: gratitude. Not as a forced emotion, not as an obligation, but as a quiet recognition of what has shaped us. Bring to mind one moment—big or small—that offered you something meaningful. A lesson, a kindness, a sense of belonging. Hold it gently in your awareness, without trying to analyze it. Just let it exist.

5. (Allow 1-2 minutes for reflection.)

6. Now, expand your awareness beyond yourself. Consider the others in this room, each holding their own moments of gratitude. Though the specifics differ, the feeling is the same. We are all connected by the experience of receiving, of appreciating, of being shaped by what has touched our lives.

7. (After 1 minute, begin to guide the group back.)

8. As we prepare to transition out of this practice, notice how gratitude feels in your body, not as a thought, but as a presence. Know that it remains with you, ready to be noticed whenever you choose to return to it. Gently bring your attention back to this space, aware of the collective energy we have created together. When you feel ready, open your eyes.

Script #81: Releasing What No Longer Serves

1. (Encourage participants to find a posture that allows both comfort and openness. Once the group is settled, begin.)

2. Take a moment to simply arrive. To let the outside world pause. To feel the presence of those around you, here with the same intention—to release, to let go, to clear space for what comes next.

3. (Pause for 30 seconds, letting the group settle.)

4. We often carry things long after they've served their purpose. Thoughts that weigh us down, emotions that linger, tension that settles into the body. Today, we sit together in the quiet act of release.

5. (Allow a breath's space before continuing.)

6. Bring to mind something you are ready to let go of. It may be small; it may be significant. Perhaps it's an expectation, a worry, a lingering doubt. Whatever it is, acknowledge it without judgment. You don't need to push it away—just recognize that it is here.

7. (Pause for 30-45 seconds.)

8. Now, imagine setting it down. Picture it gently resting—not just beside you, but in the center of our shared space. As a group, we place what we no longer need here, allowing it to be released together. As you inhale, feel the space it leaves behind. As you exhale, let the body soften, unburdened.

9. (Guide the group through 30-45 seconds of steady breaths, allowing time for this process.)

10. Though we each sit with our own experiences, we share in this act of release. Feel the quiet support of those around you—no need for words, just a presence that reminds you that you do not carry everything alone.

11. (Let the group settle into this awareness for 30-45 seconds.)

12. With your next inhale, draw in a sense of lightness. With your exhale, allow any remaining weight to dissolve. Again, inhale—renewal. Exhale—release.

13. (After 30 seconds, gently bring the meditation to a close.)

14. As we return to this space, notice how it feels to have set something down. Even if only for a moment. Know that this practice is always available to you—the simple act of acknowledging, releasing, and making space for what's next.

15. (Encourage the group to slowly open their eyes when they feel ready, carrying this sense of release with them as they move forward.)

Guided Visualizations for Groups

Guided visualizations in groups provide a creative twist by immersing participants in shared imagery. This method taps into collective creativity, turning meditation into an enjoyable and memorable journey. You can guide your group through a vivid mental landscape that encourages a sense of calm and peace. Through these shared visual journeys, connections between participants grow stronger, as everyone contributes to and partakes in the same imaginative space.

Script #82: Releasing Into the Fire

1. (Invite the group to sit comfortably, hands resting naturally. Once settled, begin.)

2. Close your eyes and take a deep breath in… and out. Let your shoulders drop, your hands rest naturally, and your breathing find a steady rhythm.

3. (Pause for 30 seconds to let the group settle.)

4. Now, picture yourself walking into an open clearing as evening sets in. In the center, a fire burns—a steady, contained flame. Around it, there are places for each of us. Take a seat, feeling the warmth of the fire in front of you, the presence of others around you.

5. (Pause.)

6. In your hands, you find an object. It represents something you are ready to let go of—perhaps a thought, a feeling, or a memory that has weighed on you. Take a moment to observe it. Notice its shape, its texture, its weight.

7. (Pause for 30-45 seconds for inner reflection.)

8. When you are ready, stand and step forward. Hold the object out toward the fire. As you release it into the flames, watch as it begins to break down. The fire absorbs it, reducing it to glowing embers, then to ash.

9. (Pause for 30 seconds.)

10. There is nothing more you need to do. The fire takes care of the rest. Allow yourself to notice any sense of relief, or simply acknowledge that the process has begun.

11. (Pause for 30 seconds.)

12. Now, take a slow breath in... and out. The fire continues to burn, steady and strong. It remains here, but our time around it is ending. As you step away, notice how you feel—perhaps lighter, perhaps clearer, or simply aware of a shift.

13. (Pause for 30-45 seconds.)

14. Begin to bring your awareness back to the present moment. Feel the support beneath you, the air around you, and the presence of others nearby. When you're ready, open your eyes.

Script #83: The Gathering Place

1. (Invite the group to find a comfortable position, ensuring their posture is relaxed yet alert. Allow them to settle into their breath.)

2. Close your eyes and begin to focus on your breath. Breathe in deeply and exhale slowly. With each breath, allow yourself to feel more present in this moment. Let go of distractions as you focus on the rhythm of your breath.

3. (Pause for 30 seconds to allow the group to settle.)

4. Imagine you are walking toward a place designed for gathering—somewhere people have come together for years to connect, share, and find stillness. This place is simple and direct. It could be an open field, a meeting room, or a space where people come to focus and center themselves. The important thing is that this space is for connection, not just with others, but with yourself.

5. (Pause to let them visualize their space.)

6. As you step into this place, you notice others here. Each person is focused, centered, and present. Some faces are familiar, others are not, but all share the same purpose: to be here, in this moment, together. There is no need to speak—just being here is enough.

7. (Pause to allow the group to absorb the feeling of presence and connection.)

8. Now, take your place among them. Notice the strength in the shared energy of the group. While each person is an individual, you are all united by the purpose of being present and connected. You don't have to do anything—just sit here and feel the strength of the group around you.

9. (Pause for 1-2 minutes and let the group settle into this feeling.)

10. Take a moment to be aware of the space—its simplicity, the quiet exchange of energy, and the focus shared between everyone here. This space is not just for today; it exists anytime you need it.

11. (Pause for a moment of reflection.)

12. When you're ready, bring your awareness back to your body and to the room. Feel the connection to yourself and to the people here with you. When you feel ready, open your eyes, bringing this sense of focus and presence with you.

Interactive Group Reflections

After the meditation, interactive group reflections can help facilitate communal learning and trust. Encouraging participants to share their experiences, insights, or feelings post-session can strengthen bonds within the group. Vulnerable sharing creates an environment of openness and acceptance, where individual members feel comfortable expressing themselves without judgment. A reflective circle, where each person has the opportunity to speak or simply listen, can be a great way to deepen understanding and empathy among group members.

Coherence Breathing for Groups

You can also incorporate coherence breathing into group sessions for different benefits. Coherence breathing is designed to bring about synchronization and relaxation within group settings. This practice involves harmonizing breath patterns, which can greatly enhance the sense of calmness and emotional regulation among participants. Focusing on coherent breathing means that group members can work toward creating an environment that promotes shared tranquility, making it a valuable tool for wellness practitioners who wish to include mindfulness techniques in their sessions.

Implementation of Coherence Breathing

Guiding a group through coherence breathing requires introducing specific implementation steps. Start by instructing participants to sit comfortably, ensuring they are relaxed but attentive. Begin with simple timing techniques, such as inhaling slowly for five seconds and exhaling for five seconds. Use verbal cues or visual aids, like images of waves, to help visualize the breath's natural ebb and flow. Alternatively, play soothing sounds or music with a steady rhythm to support this practice. These methods assist in synchronizing participants' breaths without overwhelming them.

Script #84: The Rhythmic Tide

1. (Invite the group to find a comfortable, upright position, ensuring they are relaxed but attentive. Once everyone is settled, begin.)

2. Close your eyes and take a moment to become aware of the space you share with those around you. Feel the presence of the group; each of us here for the same reason—bringing ourselves into balance, together. As you settle in, feel the steady rhythm of your breath, as natural as the waves in the ocean.

3. (Pause for 30 seconds, allowing the group to relax into the space.)

4. Now, let's begin to breathe together. Imagine that we are all part of the same ocean, each of us a wave in a steady tide. With every inhale, feel as if you are drawing in the same breath as those around you, the waves building in unity. And with every exhale, imagine those waves retreating together, moving back in sync, as if the group is one force in motion.

5. (Allow 1 minute for the group to settle into this shared rhythm.)

6. Notice the ebb and flow of our collective breath. Just like the ocean, there's no rush—no need to hurry. The waves come in

together, steady and unhurried, and they retreat in harmony. As you breathe, imagine how the entire group is moving as one, each wave supporting the other, creating a calm and constant rhythm.

7. (Pause for a few rounds of breathing, allowing the group to synchronize.)

8. As the waves rise and fall, so do we, together. Feel how each wave is part of a larger, greater movement, and how the collective rhythm strengthens the experience. Notice that with each inhale, we are connected; with each exhale, we release, together.

9. (Pause for 1 minute, giving the group time to absorb the rhythm.)

10. Now, let's take a moment to become aware of the stillness that follows the waves. As the water retreats, there is a space of calm, a quiet moment between the movement. This stillness is shared by the group—each of us moving together, finding peace in the space between the waves.

11. (Pause for 1-2 minutes, allowing the group to fully engage with the idea of collective calm.)

12. When you're ready, let your attention move back to the room and space around you. Feel the group around you, the connection, and the shared rhythm we've created. As you open your eyes, carry with you the sense of unity and calm that we've experienced together.

Incorporating Ambient Soundscapes

Ambient soundscapes are an integral part of setting the mood for meditation. These soundscapes promote calmness and sharpen concentration. Unlike sound healing instruments, which are often used as focal points, ambient sounds tend to blend into the background, helping participants drift into meditative states without abrupt interruptions. Some examples of ambient soundscapes you can incorporate include:

- **Nature Sounds**: Gentle rain, ocean waves, rustling leaves, flowing rivers, distant thunder, or chirping birds can create a grounding and tranquil environment.

- **White, Pink, and Brown Noise**: White noise provides a consistent, neutral hum, while pink noise (e.g., steady rainfall or wind through trees) has a softer, more natural tone. Brown noise, which has deeper, richer frequencies (e.g., rolling thunder or strong ocean waves), is often used to enhance relaxation.

- **Singing Bowls and Chimes**: Tibetan singing bowls, crystal bowls, and soft chimes produce resonant frequencies that promote deep relaxation and energy balance.

- **Binaural Beats and Isochronic Tones**: These specially designed sound frequencies stimulate the brain's natural rhythms, aiding in deep focus, relaxation, or even lucid dreaming states.

- **Soft Instrumental Music**: Slow, flowing melodies from pianos, harps, flutes, or string instruments help foster a serene atmosphere.

- **Sacred Sounds and Mantras**: Repetitive mantras like "Om," "So Hum," or Buddhist chanting serve as both auditory and energetic anchors.

- **Space and Cosmic Sounds**: Subtle synth tones, ethereal drones, or recordings of deep-space frequencies (such as NASA's cosmic soundscapes) create an expansive, open feeling conducive to transcendental meditation.

- **Fire and Hearth Sounds**: The crackling of a fireplace or a softly burning campfire brings a sense of warmth, comfort, and presence.

Bringing It All Together

Group meditations open up a whole new world of possibilities for participants to explore their inner selves while connecting with others. Throughout this chapter, we looked at different ways to make these meditations more engaging and impactful, using techniques like dynamic group energy meditations, themed sessions, guided visualizations, and interactive reflections. Each method comes with its own unique charm, whether it's sharing synchronized breaths, diving into creative visualization, or engaging in themed discussions that resonate deeply with each participant. These experiences make group meditation about building a collective experience that nurtures and supports everyone involved.

Chapter 10:

Themes and Intentions in Guided

Practices

Crafting scripts around specific themes and intentions for targeted outcomes is a process that can transform any meditation practice. Whether you're leading a meditation session, yoga class, or coaching meeting, setting intentions drives the entire experience by helping participants focus their energy and attention in a way that feels both meaningful and rewarding. Taking this kind of intentional approach encourages mindfulness and allows participants to tap into deeper layers of self-awareness and personal growth.

The chapter will dive into the mechanics of crafting these scripts with precision and care, as well as various scripts designed for different themes and ideas that you can share to make the scripts you offer more varied and beneficial. You'll find insights on how to tailor meditation and visualization sessions to address diverse needs, like stress relief, personal growth, or finding inner calm. We'll also talk about different techniques to elevate themed and intention-based practices. All these elements together provide a comprehensive look at how thoughtful themes and intentions can turn guided practices into incredible experiences.

Setting Intentions in Meditation

Intention setting in meditation practices is great for enhancing focus and declaring purpose, which are central to any fruitful meditation session. With clear intentions, practitioners know what they aim to explore or achieve during their meditation sessions. Unlike goals, which are often tangible and outcome-oriented, intentions are more about the mindset and the energy one brings into the practice.

Having an intention aligns the mind's focus and helps tether fleeting thoughts to a central theme, be it cultivating gratitude, building resilience, or discovering a sense of stillness. This practice encourages staying present and attentive, which can significantly enhance the meditative experience and lead to deeper insights.

Examples of Intentions

Different types of intentions address diverse needs. For example, someone aiming for personal growth might set an intention centered on self-acceptance in order to affirm daily actions that support self-love and authenticity. On the other hand, those seeking stress relief may focus on intentions that emphasize letting go of tension and embracing relaxation. Guiding those you work with to articulate these varied intentions helps personalize meditation sessions and makes them more impactful.

Challenges in Setting Intentions

However, participants may experience challenges like clarity in defining intentions or emotional resistance that hinder the process. It's not uncommon for people to struggle with identifying what truly matters to them or confronting emotions that arise during meditation. Here, empathy and guidance become essential. To overcome this, be sure to offer a supportive space where practitioners feel safe to explore their intentions without judgment. Open dialogues about these challenges can create greater understanding and encourage persistence despite the hurdles. Such discussions might involve gently prompting questions like, "What does peace look like to you today?" or "In what areas do you seek growth?" This supportive environment helps individuals navigate through uncertainty and embrace vulnerability in their journey.

Despite potential obstacles, the adaptability of intention setting stands as one of its most compelling features. As people evolve, so too do their intentions. These intentions can be continuously revised and refined to reflect one's current state of being and aspirations.

Script #85: Rooting Into Intention

Setting intentions can seem challenging, even before a meditation. At the same time, meditating on one's intentions can help clarify them and bring true values to the surface. This meditation script is designed for you to share with participants in order to help create a stronger awareness of their intentions, both for themselves and for you as the facilitator.

1. (Invite participants to find a comfortable seated position, ensuring they are relaxed but attentive. Allow a few moments for everyone to settle before beginning.)

2. Close your eyes and take a slow, steady breath in through your nose... and release it gently through your mouth. Feel the air as it enters, expanding your ribs, filling the space within you. And as you exhale, let go of any tension, any expectation—simply arrive here, in this moment.

3. (Pause for 1 minute.)

4. As you continue to breathe, turn your attention inward. Beneath the surface of thoughts, beneath the noise of daily life, there is a quiet space within you—a place where clarity lives. Without forcing, without searching, allow yourself to rest here.

5. (Pause for 1 minute.)

6. Now, I invite you to consider a question: "What do you want to bring into this space?" Not as a goal to achieve, not as a task to complete, but as a way of being. What energy, what presence do you wish to cultivate in yourself today?

7. (Pause for 1 minute.)

8. There is no right answer, only what feels true to you in this moment. Perhaps you wish to invite patience. Maybe curiosity.

Resilience. Gratitude. Or simply stillness. Whatever arises, allow it to take shape in your mind—not as a demand, but as a gentle offering to yourself.

9. (Pause.)

10. If words come, let them form a simple phrase—an intention you can hold lightly, like a whisper within you. If no words come, that's okay too. The feeling alone is enough.

11. (Pause for 1 minute.)

12. Now, with your next breath in, draw this intention deeper into yourself. Imagine it settling into your breath, your body, your awareness. And as you exhale, let it extend outward—into this space, into the day ahead.

13. (Allow for another 30-45 seconds.)

14. As we begin to close this practice, know that your intention does not stay confined to this moment. It walks with you. It will shape itself within your actions, your words, and your choices. You do not need to force it—simply allow it to be present, like a quiet guide.

15. (Pause for 30 seconds, then gently guide participants to return to the present space.)

16. Bring your awareness back to the room. Notice the rhythm of your breath, the weight of your body where it rests. When you feel ready, open your eyes, carrying your intention forward with you.

Themed Visualizations and Journeys

Themed visualizations can significantly improve meditative experiences by providing deeper emotional connections and relaxation for participants. Using themes like nature or healing journeys can help you create a vivid mental environment that invites participants to explore, relax, and connect on a more meaningful and valuable level. Nature-based themes, for example, might involve envisioning a serene forest with whispering trees or a gentle stream, while healing journeys could guide clients through personal growth narratives, encouraging emotional release and rejuvenation.

Guiding Clients Through Journeys

Effective descriptive language is necessary in guiding these visualizations. The choice of words sets the tone and pace that helps those you work with fully immerse themselves in the experience. Slow, deliberate descriptions mean that participants can build detailed mental images that lead to a sense of presence and engagement.

Creating Engaging Scenarios

Crafting engaging scenarios that work with multiple senses can further improve the experience. For example, you can try incorporating auditory elements like the sound of ocean waves, birdsong, or a light breeze, which can be imagined alongside the visual storyline. These sounds help ground participants in the scene, as well as provide context and depth that enrich their immersion. Also, suggesting physical sensations, like feeling a soft breeze or the texture of sand beneath one's feet, can deepen the connection to the visualization.

Evaluating Client Responses

Something else to consider is how your clients respond to different sessions, which can aid in refining future sessions. After each visualization, it's helpful to evaluate how participants felt during the experience and what impact it had on them, which you can find out by having an open conversation about the experience. Were there parts where they felt particularly engaged or moments they found distracting? Gathering this information can help you tailor future meditations to better meet client needs, enhance effectiveness, and ensure continual improvement. It also encourages reflection among clients.

Themed Visualization Scripts

With all of these elements in mind, let's take a look at two themed visualization scripts that you can share with those you work with.

Script #86: The Garden of Reflection

1. Find a comfortable position, sitting or lying down. Gently let your eyelids close and inhale deeply through your nose before exhaling gently through your mouth. As you do so, feel the tension seeping out of your body.

2. (Pause.)

3. Now, imagine walking into a peaceful garden. The ground beneath you is soft yet steady. A light breeze moves through the trees, and the air feels fresh. This space is yours—a quiet place to pause and reconnect.

4. (Pause.)

5. As you walk, notice the colors and scents of the flowers around you. Each bloom represents something you want to cultivate: strength, peace, clarity, or creativity. Choose one that speaks to you. Imagine inhaling its scent, breathing in that quality, allowing it to settle within you.

6. (Pause for 30 seconds.)

7. Ahead, you see a bench in a quiet corner. Take a seat and let yourself be fully supported. As you sit, take a moment to simply be. Let your breath slow, your body relax. There is nothing to do, nothing to fix—just a chance to sit in quiet awareness. Now, take a moment to reflect on what you need

most—calm, focus, ease, or something else. There's nothing to force or figure out—just notice what arises.

8. (Pause for 1-2 minutes.)

9. After a few breaths, notice how you feel. Perhaps a sense of calm, clarity, or steadiness has emerged. Whatever is present, acknowledge it, knowing you can return to this feeling whenever you need.

10. (Pause for 30 seconds.)

11. When you're ready, stand and walk back along the path, carrying with you the clarity and steadiness you've found. Feel your breath, your body, the energy you've gathered.

12. (Pause for 30 seconds.)

13. Slowly return to the present moment. Notice the weight of your body, the rhythm of your breath. When you're ready, open your eyes, bringing this sense of calm with you.

Script #87: The Clear Room

1. Sit in a comfortable position, allowing your breath to settle into a natural rhythm. Take a deep breath in, and slowly exhale, letting go of any tension you might be holding.

2. (Pause.)

3. Imagine yourself in a clean, quiet room. The walls are neutral, and the space feels open and uncluttered. There is a sense of calm here, with plenty of room to think and breathe.

4. (Pause for 30 seconds.)

5. Take a moment to notice the space around you. The room is quiet, with soft light coming through a window. There is no rush, no distractions—only the simplicity of the space that invites you to be present.

6. Pause for 45-60 seconds.)

7. With each breath, feel yourself becoming more centered in this room. If any thoughts or distractions arise, simply acknowledge them and let them pass, without holding onto them. The room is neutral and calm, offering you the space to just be.

8. (Pause for 1-2 minutes to allow stillness.)

9. If there's something on your mind that you've been carrying, imagine setting it down on a table in the corner of the room. It's no longer your concern here. The room remains clear, and so can your mind.

10. (Pause for 1 minute.)

11. Now, in this space, take a moment to check in with yourself. What do you need at this moment? Simply observe—there is no need to rush to a solution, just space to listen to your thoughts without distraction.

12. (Pause for 1 minute.)

13. When you feel ready, return to your breath and your body. Slowly begin to bring your awareness back to the present, carrying with you the clarity and calm of the room. When you're ready, open your eyes.

Seasonal and Environmental Themes

Incorporating seasonal and environmental themes into meditation practices can elevate the experience by aligning it with natural cycles. This approach makes use of the energies and characteristics unique to each season, which can help those you work with develop a meaningful, healing connection to nature. Let's dive into how different thematic scripts can enhance meditation sessions and support specific emotional and psychological needs throughout the year.

Scripts for New Beginnings and Renewal (Spring)

Spring is synonymous with new beginnings and renewal. When working with meditation scripts for this season, focus on themes of growth and optimism. The energy of spring invites us to embrace rejuvenation, similar to the way nature bursts back to life after the stillness of winter. Emphasizing renewal and fresh starts helps spring meditations nurture an attitude of positivity and hopefulness.

Script #88: The Seed of Growth

1. Find a comfortable position, either seated or lying down. Allow your body to settle, feeling fully supported. If it feels right for you, gently close your eyes.

2. (Pause.)

3. Take a slow, deep breath in through your nose. Feel your lungs expand as they fill with air. Then allow yourself to release the air softly through your mouth, releasing any tension you may be holding as you exhale. With each breath, feel yourself becoming more mindful of the present.

4. (Pause for 45 seconds to let the breath deepen.)

5. Now, bring your awareness to the idea of growth. Imagine the changing seasons—how winter gradually gives way to spring. The earth softens, the air warms, and nature begins to awaken.

6. (Pause.)

7. Picture a small seed resting in the soil. It is held gently beneath the surface, not buried, but protected. This seed contains everything it needs to grow, and when the time is right, it begins to awaken. This seed symbolizes you—acknowledge the potential already within you.

8. (Pause.)

9. Now, take a moment to reflect. What area of your life is ready for renewal? What is beginning to take shape within you? There is no need to have all the answers—just an openness to possibility. Trust that growth happens in its own time.

10. (Allow 1-2 minutes for personal reflection.)

11. As you breathe, connect with this process. Just as the seed follows its path, you are also evolving in your own way. Trust in this journey. There is no need to force change; it unfolds as it should.

12. (Allow 30-45 seconds to integrate this message.)

13. When you are ready, begin to bring your awareness back to the present. Feel the surface beneath you, the rhythm of your breath. Gently move different parts of your body as you allow yourself to reconnect with the present moment.

14. (Pause.)

15. Take one final deep breath in. As you exhale, carry with you the quiet confidence that growth is always happening, in its own time and in its own way.

16. When you feel ready, open your eyes.

Script #89: The Clarity of Spring

1. Take a moment to settle into a comfortable position, allowing your body to relax. Notice the natural rhythm of your breath—each inhale bringing in calm, each exhale releasing any tension you might be holding.

2. (Pause for 30 seconds.)

3. Now, imagine it's a clear spring morning. The air is fresh and cool, with just enough warmth to feel comfortable. The sky above is open and clear, with no distractions. It's a simple, calm scene that brings a sense of clarity.

4. (Pause.)

5. Let yourself feel your feet grounded in their current space. The earth beneath you is solid and steady, supporting you as you stand or sit. There is no rush, no pressure to move forward quickly. Everything is constantly in its place. You can take your time.

6. (Pause for 45 seconds to deepen the grounding.)

7. As you breathe in, notice the simplicity of the moment. There are no demands, just a quiet presence. The world around you is moving forward at its own pace, shifting slowly from the colder months into the freshness of spring. You can feel that quiet shift within yourself, too. There's no need to force change, but you can feel it happening, gently, at the right time.

8. (Pause for 30 seconds.)

9. In this space, there is clarity. No distractions, no rushing. Just the quiet certainty that things are moving forward, whether seen or not. Allow yourself to be a part of that, knowing you are exactly where you need to be.

10. (Pause for 30-45 seconds.)

11. As you continue to breathe, let the steady rhythm of the world around you remind you that you can handle change in your own time, with no urgency. What is needed will come when it's ready, just as spring brings new growth at its own pace. You don't need to push, just allow yourself to be.

12. (Pause for 30-45 seconds.)

13. When you feel ready, bring your awareness back to your body, your breath, and the space you're in. As you open your eyes, carry with you the quiet strength and patience of spring. Change is happening, and you are part of it.

Scripts for Letting Go and Transformation (Autumn)

Autumn scripts, on the other hand, focus on letting go and transformation. As leaves fall and trees prepare for dormancy, autumn is a great reminder of life's impermanence and the beauty of change. In meditation, this season can become a time for processing and accepting transitions. Participants can meditate on the idea of release—letting go of old habits, grudges, or fears that no longer serve them. Concentrating on acceptance and finding peace during change means they can find space for liberation and growth. Autumn inspires reflection on what needs to be released and what needs to be nurtured. Visualization techniques might include the image of leaves gracefully falling, symbolizing the shedding of unnecessary burdens (Telford, 2023).

Script #90: The Autumn Path of Reflection

1. Find a comfortable position where your body feels fully supported. Allow your breath to flow naturally. With each inhale, welcome a sense of calm. With each exhale, release any tension, letting it drift away.

2. (Pause for 30 seconds to let the body settle.)

3. Now, imagine yourself standing at the start of a calm path, surrounded by trees in the midst of autumn. The leaves have turned deep red, burnt orange, and soft yellow—a quiet reminder of change. The ground beneath you is steady, and the world feels still, as if nature itself is pausing to reflect.

4. (Pause.)

5. As you begin to walk, notice the leaves beneath your feet. They crunch softly with each step. These fallen leaves represent the past: experiences, thoughts, and emotions that have shaped you. Some have served their purpose, their journey complete.

6. Take a moment to reflect. What are you ready to let go of? Are there habits, worries, or beliefs that no longer serve you? There

is no need to force anything—just notice what comes to mind. Like the leaves drifting from the branches, release happens naturally when the time is right.

7. (Pause for 45 seconds of reflection.)

8. As you continue walking, feel the openness that letting go creates. The trees stand tall and steady, unshaken by change. Even as they shed what is no longer needed, their roots remain strong. You, too, are steady. You, too, are whole.

9. (Pause.)

10. A gentle breeze moves through the trees, carrying away what is ready to leave. It reminds you that change is not an ending but a quiet preparation for what's ahead. With each breath, feel yourself making space—welcoming renewal, embracing transformation.

11. (Pause 1 minute.)

12. When you feel ready, draw your attention to the pace of your breathing. Feel the surface beneath you, the rhythm of your inhales and exhales. Carry this sense of clarity with you, knowing that release creates space for growth.

13. (Pause for 30-45 seconds.)

14. When you are ready, open your eyes.

Script #91: The Harvest of Autumn

1. Settle into a position of comfort, allowing your breath to deepen and slow. With each inhale, invite in the fresh, earthy scent of autumn, and with each exhale, release any tension or lingering heaviness, creating space within you.

2. (Pause for 20 seconds.)

3. Now, imagine yourself walking through a quiet orchard, where the trees are heavy with ripe fruit. The sky is a soft blue, and a gentle breeze rustles the leaves, their colors deepening with the season's change. The ground beneath you is firm, but you can feel the softness of fallen leaves underfoot, a reminder that the earth is in its own cycle of transition.

4. (Pause for 30 seconds to let the image settle.)

5. In your hands, you hold a basket—a symbol of your inner world. As you walk through the orchard, you begin to gather fruit, each piece representing something in your life. Some fruit is ripe and full of sweetness—these are the things that have nourished you, brought you joy, or helped you grow. You place them gently in your basket, recognizing their value.

6. (Pause for 45-60 seconds.)

7. Then, you come across fruit that is bruised or overripe—these are the burdens or thoughts that have become too heavy or no longer serve you. You can feel the weight of them, and yet, there is no need to hold onto them any longer. You set these down, watching them roll off your path, knowing that by letting go, you are making space for new growth.

8. (Pause for 45-60 seconds.)

9. Continue gathering what is ready to be collected—what still nourishes and strengthens you—and letting go of what no longer serves its purpose.

10. (Pause for 45 seconds.)

11. As you finish gathering, you take a moment to appreciate the harvest—the things you've kept, the lessons, the connections, the memories, and the growth. You walk forward, feeling lighter, more focused, and ready to step into the next season.

12. (Pause for 45 seconds.)

13. Slowly begin to bring your awareness back to your body, back to your breath. Feel your feet on the ground, the support beneath you, and when you're ready, gently open your eyes, carrying with you the sense of renewal and readiness for the season ahead.

Scripts for Grounding and Warmth (Winter)

Winter brings a different energy with its themes of grounding, warmth, and inner stillness. During this season, meditation practices can emphasize introspection and rest. Winter's quiet and subdued nature mirrors the opportunity to turn inward and reconnect with one's core self. Sessions focusing on inner reflection, self-discovery, and the importance of rest can help combat feelings of isolation or stagnation that may arise during colder months.

Script #92: The Winter Pause

1. Find a comfortable position where your body can relax fully. Take a deep breath in, feeling the cool, crisp air filling your lungs. As you exhale, gently release any tension you're holding, allowing your body to soften with each breath.

2. (Pause.)

3. Now, imagine yourself standing in a peaceful winter landscape. The world around you is quiet, the ground covered in fresh, untouched snow. The air is cool but gentle, and you feel the stillness wrapping around you, inviting you to pause and slow down.

4. (Pause for a few slow breaths.)

5. Take a moment to appreciate the calm of the season. Winter offers a space for rest, reflection, and renewal. There is no need to rush; only the quiet presence of the moment allowing you to simply be.

6. (Allow 30-45 seconds to let the body absorb the stillness.)

7. As you stand in this peaceful place, you notice a warm, inviting light in the distance. You begin to walk toward it, drawn by the soft glow. Soon, you find yourself entering a small room where a fire burns gently in the fireplace. The warmth from the fire spreads through the space, soothing your body and calming your mind.

8. (Pause.)

9. Sit for a moment in this quiet warmth. Feel the support beneath you, allowing your body to rest fully, knowing that in this space, you are safe to pause. There is no need to do anything—simply to be present in this moment. Let the warmth and stillness of winter wash over you, offering peace and comfort.

10. (Pause here for 2-3 minutes.)

11. When you're ready, gently bring your awareness back to the present. Feel the support around you and the calm you have found within. Open your eyes, knowing that stillness and rest are always within reach whenever you need them.

Script #93: Winter's Gentle Rhythm

1. Close your eyes and take a slow, steady breath in. Feel the air move through you—cool as it enters, warm as you release it. Let each breath draw you further into stillness, softening any tension.

2. (Allow for 30 seconds to anchor into stillness.)

3. Now, imagine a winter sky—pale and soft, stretching endlessly above. The world is quiet, the season moving at its own unhurried pace. Nothing is frozen in time; everything is simply slow, steady, patient.

4. (Let the image form and deepen.)

5. In this moment, you are part of that rhythm. Like the subtle shift of clouds or the distant sound of wind, your breath moves in and out without effort.

6. (Pause for 30-45 seconds.)

7. There's no need to push forward. Winter teaches us that rest is not a pause from growth—it is part of it. Beneath the surface, there is quiet preparation, energy gathering like roots resting beneath the frost.

8. (Pause for 30-45 seconds.)

9. With each inhale, sense a quiet strength growing within you. With each exhale, let go of the need to hurry or force.

10. (Pause for 1-2 minutes.)

11. You are exactly where you need to be.

12. (Let this affirmation settle fully.)

13. Rest in this stillness for a few moments longer, knowing that this slow season has a purpose—and so do you.

14. (Pause for 1-2 minutes.)

15. Finally, when you feel ready, gently bring your mind back to the room we're in without rushing yourself. Wiggle your fingers, feel the ground beneath you, and open your eyes softly, carrying with you the quiet strength of winter's rhythm.

Scripts for Energy and Transformation (Summer)

Summer scripts focus on harnessing the vibrant energy of the season to promote personal growth and transformation. The long days and warm weather inspire a sense of freedom and vitality, making it the perfect time to embrace change. These meditations encourage participants to explore new possibilities, take bold steps forward, and tap into their inner strength.

Themes of exploration, creativity, and resilience are woven throughout, inviting participants to reflect on their personal journey and where they are headed. Summer meditations can include visualizations of movement and fluidity, such as flowing rivers or expansive skies, symbolizing expansion. The focus is on embracing new opportunities with a sense of excitement and optimism.

Script #94: Summer of Strength and Progress

1. Settle into a position that feels most comfortable for you, and then let your eyes close softly. Begin to focus on your breath—slow and steady. With each inhale, feel your lungs fill completely, and with each exhale, feel any tension begin to release. Allow your body to settle, letting go of any distractions, and bring your full attention to the present moment.

2. (Pause for 45-60 seconds.)

3. Summer is a time for action. It's a time to build, to grow, and to move forward with purpose. In this meditation, you will focus on the strength and progress that comes from consistent effort and clear intention.

4. (Pause briefly, about 30 seconds, to transition focus.)

5. Let your attention focus on how your body feels in the here and now. Notice how it feels right now—steady, grounded, and capable. With every breath, feel the solid foundation of your body supporting you as you move through life. Summer is a time to harness that energy, to take action, and to expand into new opportunities. Feel that strength already within you.

6. (Pause for 1-1.5 minutes.)

7. Now, think about an area of your life where you want to see real progress. This could be a project, a personal goal, or a

change you'd like to make. Whatever it is, bring it clearly to mind. Picture yourself making steady progress in this area—taking small but consistent steps toward your goal. See yourself handling obstacles with confidence, finding solutions when challenges arise, and moving forward with a steady determination.

8. (Allow 1-3 minutes for personal visualization.)

9. As you visualize this process, notice how you feel. There is no rush, no need to hurry—just the steady, reliable momentum of progress. Every step you take brings you closer to where you want to be. Summer is about staying focused, making clear decisions, and trusting the process. With each effort, you are expanding what is possible for you. You are building something strong and lasting.

10. (Let participants reflect for 1-1.5 minutes.)

11. As this image becomes clearer, feel the energy of summer filling you with purpose and resolve. This energy doesn't need to be complicated or overwhelming—it's simply about showing up, day after day, and doing the work. And each day, you grow stronger, more capable, and more confident in your ability to achieve your goals.

12. (Let this idea take root for 45-60 seconds.)

13. Take a moment to reflect on your ability to expand. Summer is a time of possibility, of pushing beyond the limits of what you thought was possible. Your capacity for growth is greater than you realize. With every action you take, you are expanding into the next level of your potential.

14. (Pause for 1-1.5 minutes.)

15. When you feel ready, start to focus on the flow of your breathing, without forcing it to change. Begin to reconnect with the space around you, and when you feel ready, slowly open your eyes. Take with you the understanding that progress is

built one step at a time, and you have the strength to make it happen.

Script #95: Abundance and Limitless Growth

1. Sit comfortably, close your eyes, and take a deep breath. Inhale slowly, filling your lungs completely, then exhale, allowing your body to relax with each breath. Let yourself settle into the moment.

2. (Let the body and mind arrive.)

3. Summer is a time of abundance, a season full of life, energy, and growth. In this space, feel the abundance that surrounds you and flows through you. It's a time to acknowledge the natural growth within you, the potential that is always present, waiting to be realized.

4. (Pause for 30-45 seconds.)

5. See yourself in a space where everything around you is flourishing—plants are growing, the air is warm and full of life. Just the steady growth of nature and life unfolding. Notice how expansive this feels, how much there is to be grateful for in this moment. You don't need to push or strive; you are simply part of this life's flow.

6. (Allow 30-45 seconds to fully visualize.)

7. Now, bring to mind an area in your life where you feel you could grow or expand. It could be in your relationships, your work, or even your own personal growth. See this area clearly in your mind, knowing that it holds infinite potential. Just as the world around you is abundant, so too is this space in your life.

8. (Pause for 1-3 minutes.)

9. There is plenty of room for you to grow and expand in your own unique way. You are part of this larger abundance, and it is within your reach.

10. (Pause for 45-60 seconds.)

11. Take a moment to appreciate the sense of growth that is already happening within you, even if you can't always see it. Trust that you are growing in ways that matter, in ways that support your journey.

12. (Pause for 1-1.5 minutes.)

13. When you're ready, pull your attention back to the sensations of your body. Feel your breath moving through you, and slowly reconnect with your surroundings. Open your eyes, carrying with you the sense of abundance and growth that summer has to offer.

Spiritual Themes

Spiritual themes often involve guiding clients to visualize themselves in alignment with universal energies or exploring their life's purpose within the context of greater cosmic forces. Integrating such themes means you can help those you work with harness a sense of belonging to something larger than themselves, all while enhancing their capacity for mindfulness. This heightened awareness promotes peace, stability, and the ability to navigate life's challenges with grace.

Script #96: The Thread of Existence

1. Close your eyes and find a comfortable position. Take a deep breath in, filling your lungs, and then slowly exhale, letting your body relax with each breath. With every inhale, feel yourself grounded in this moment. With each exhale, feel any tension release.

2. (Pause for 45-60 seconds.)

3. You are here now. And yet, you are also connected to something much larger, something that exists beyond time and space, something that has always been, and will always be.

4. (Let the concept expand gently.)

5. Picture yourself standing in an open space—no walls, no boundaries—only connection. This is a space where everything, past and future, is woven together in a continuous flow. You've never had to search for this place because you've always been a part of it.

6. (Pause for 30-45 seconds.)

7. Before you, a thread appears. It's not just a simple strand, but something deeper, alive, filled with energy. This thread holds the stories of the past, the potential of the future, and everything in between. As you feel its presence, you sense it is not separate from you—it is intertwined with your being, part of you, an inseparable connection.

8. (Allow 30-60 seconds to fully sense the imagery.)

9. As you follow the thread, it moves with you, showing you glimpses of your life, your choices, and your purpose. The thread does not judge, does not break, and does not tangle. It simply flows, adapting, evolving, always moving forward as part of a larger design. It leads you through moments of joy and moments of challenge, and with every step, you realize that each experience has shaped you, and each path has been a part of the ongoing weave of your existence.

10. (Let this reflection deepen for 1-2 minutes.)

11. Standing in this awareness, you feel the thread deeply intertwined within you. There's nothing you need to force, nothing to grasp. You have always belonged.

12. (Let the message settle fully for 1 minute.)

13. Now, bring your attention back to your breath, back to the sensations in your body, reconnecting with the present moment. But remember, the thread remains with you, ever-present, always guiding you, always part of you.

14. (Pause for 30-45 seconds as participants slowly reconnect with physical awareness.)

15. When you're ready, slowly open your eyes, carrying with you the understanding that you are connected, always part of the greater whole.

Emotional Themes

On the emotional front, processing grief and loss through guided meditation can provide much-needed support during difficult times that your clients may experience. Emotional themes offer solace and understanding by creating a safe space where participants can explore their feelings without judgment.

Emotional themes designed around the acceptance of grief encourage clients to not only feel their emotions but also recognize their potential. Grief-focused meditations aid people in honoring and moving through grief, developing resilience along the way (Archer, n.d.). This process can be intensely liberating and help with dissolving emotional blockages that may have been preventing clients from moving forward.

Script #97: Honoring the Weight of Grief

1. While you begin your session, take a second to get in touch with your body, relaxing any areas of tension. Find a comfortable position where you can feel grounded, allowing yourself to be present in this moment without judgment. We're not here to rush or fix anything, but simply to honor the emotions that arise.

2. (Let the body settle for 45-60 seconds.)

3. Bring your awareness inward, not to change anything, but to observe. You may notice a heaviness, a tightness, or perhaps a space of emptiness. Whatever it is, meet it with acceptance, as it is. There is no right or wrong way to feel grief.

4. (Pause for 45-60 seconds.)

5. Allow your breath to flow in and out gently, noticing how your body responds. Each inhale can be a soft acknowledgment of your emotions. Each exhale can be a moment of letting go, not to eliminate grief but to create space for it. Allow it to be as it is.

6. (Pause for 1-1.5 minutes.)

7. Imagine the grief as a weight in your chest, perhaps dense and uncomfortable. Without rushing to remove it, let your attention rest on it. What does it feel like? Is it sharp, heavy, or dull? Notice the sensations without labeling or trying to change them. Let them simply exist. You are not the grief itself; it is something you carry, but you are not consumed by it.

8. (Pause for 1.5-2 minutes for deep sensing and awareness.)

9. Sit with the weight for a moment. There is no hurry here. As you breathe, consider how this grief has shaped you. What has it taught you? What has it taken from you? Give yourself permission to feel all the complexity of these answers.

10. (Allow 2-3 minutes for reflection.)

11. When you're ready, gently release your focus on the weight, knowing that it will return, and that is okay. You have given it the space it needs. You do not need to carry it alone. In time, it may soften, shift, or change. But for now, simply honor its presence.

12. (Pause for 45-60 seconds. Let this message land.)

13. Take a few more breaths. Slowly return to the room, carrying with you the understanding that grief is not an enemy to fight but an experience to be met with compassion. You are allowed to feel it fully, and through that, you allow yourself to heal.

Script #98: Grief as a Transformative Companion

1. As you settle into this practice, take a moment to reflect on the intention behind this meditation. You are not here to erase your grief, but to create a compassionate space for it to reveal its transformative power. Feel free to let go of any distractions, knowing that you are here, in this moment, with your emotions.

2. (Pause for 45-60 seconds to allow full arrival.)

3. Begin by noticing the sensation of your body in this space. How does it feel to be here, right now? With each breath you take, become aware of any sensations that accompany your grief—whether it feels like tension, weight, or perhaps a quiet sorrow. Whatever form it takes, let it be, without the need to understand it fully just yet.

4. (Allow 60-75 seconds for gentle scanning and observation.)

5. Now, acknowledge the grief as a companion on your journey. It has been with you for a reason, and while it may feel heavy, it has been helping you process, reflect, and remember. Grief is a silent teacher, guiding you through your emotions with wisdom you may not fully grasp in this moment. But that is okay. It will reveal itself in time.

6. (Let this reflection settle in for 1-1.5 minutes.)

7. Feel how your breath carries you, not away from the grief, but alongside it. With each inhale, notice how the weight shifts or changes. With each exhale, allow the grief to move through you, not as something to avoid, but as something you can endure. As you breathe, silently repeat the affirmation: "I honor

this grief. I accept it as part of my healing. I trust that it will transform, just as I will."

8. (Pause for 1-3 minutes to repeat the affirmation silently.)

9. Allow yourself to sit with this knowing: grief does not have to be a burden. It can be a catalyst for growth. When you are ready, release your focus on the sensation, knowing you have given it the attention it deserves and that you are not trapped by it.

10. (Let this insight integrate for 1 minute.)

11. Breathe in and out deeply as you pull your awareness gently back to the present moment. Know that your grief is part of your healing journey, and through acceptance, you create the space to move forward in your own time, at your own pace. You are not alone in this process.

Inner Strength and Adaptability

Inner strength is more than endurance—it is the ability to adapt, grow, and remain steady in the face of change. Challenges often bring uncertainty, and resilience comes not just from standing firm but from staying flexible and adjusting with confidence.

Cultivating adaptability helps individuals embrace change rather than resist it. Through mindful practices, they learn to reframe fear as courage and view challenges as opportunities for personal growth. Instead of seeing obstacles as roadblocks, they begin to recognize them as pathways to greater self-awareness and transformation.

True inner strength is not rigid; it is fluid and responsive, allowing individuals to navigate setbacks with a constructive mindset. Developing both resilience and adaptability means that we can meet life's uncertainties with clarity, confidence, and a deep trust in our own capacity to thrive.

Script #99: Connecting With Your Inner Strength

1. Welcome to this moment of pause and reflection. In this space, you're not searching for something outside of yourself, but rather reconnecting with the strength that lies within you, the strength that you have always had, even in moments when you couldn't see it.

2. Start by focusing your attention on how your body feels in the present moment. Feel the weight of your body where it touches the surface beneath you. Notice how the ground supports you. In the same way, your inner strength has always supported you through every challenge, even if you weren't always aware of it.

3. (Let participants settle into physical awareness for 45-60 seconds.)

4. Take a deep breath in, and as you exhale, release any tension you may be holding. Feel your body relax with each breath. With every inhale, you invite calmness; with every exhale, you release what no longer serves you or your life.

5. Pause for 60-75 seconds of slow breathing and release.)

6. As you settle into the present moment, think of a time when you faced a difficult situation. Remember the feelings you had, the uncertainty, the challenge. But notice, too, that you survived. You moved through that moment, and you are here now, stronger for having experienced it.

7. (Allow time to reflect on the memory for 1-1.5 minutes.)

8. Take a moment to think of a situation where you discovered a strength you weren't aware of before. Perhaps it was in a moment of challenge or a time of change. What did you learn about yourself in that experience? What inner resources did you tap into? Allow yourself to feel that strength now, letting it rise within you, like a steady force that has always been part of who you are.

9. (Pause for 2-3 minutes.)

10. As you continue to breathe deeply, think about any challenges you may be facing now, or even those you might encounter in the future. Rather than seeing them as obstacles, see them as opportunities for growth. You are capable of navigating each one. Breathe in the confidence to face what comes, and breathe out any doubt or fear.

11. (Let confidence settle in for 1-1.5 minutes.)

12. Know that your strength is not defined by the absence of difficulty, but by your ability to meet life's challenges with courage and wisdom. With each challenge, you grow. With each moment, you become more attuned to the inner resources you already possess.

13. (Pause for 30-45 seconds to integrate this reflection.)

14. Take a few more breaths, grounding yourself in the knowledge that you are stronger than you think. You are capable. When you're ready, gently open your eyes, carrying with you the awareness of your own inner strength.

Self-Worth and Confidence

Building self-worth and confidence through guided practices helps individuals recognize and honor their intrinsic value. By embracing themes that focus on self-empowerment and acknowledging personal strengths, participants can develop a solid foundation of self-assurance. Practices that encourage affirmations of self-worth and positive self-reflection are particularly effective in fostering this growth. Encouraging individuals to recognize and celebrate their unique qualities, while practicing kindness toward themselves, reinforces their belief in their abilities and boosts their confidence. Over time, these practices help to create a resilient mindset, allowing individuals to confidently navigate life with a strong sense of self and purpose.

Script #100: Embracing Self-Worth and Confidence

1. In this practice, you will create space for you to connect with your inherent value. This moment is an opportunity to gently strengthen your sense of self-worth and build your inner foundation of confidence. There is no need to change anything—simply notice what arises and allow yourself to be present with it.

2. Take a deep breath and settle into the space you occupy. Feel the support beneath you, whether you're sitting or lying down. Let yourself relax into the moment, allowing your body to soften. Notice how you are supported, just as you are, without needing to prove anything.

3. (Let the body ease into rest for 45-60 seconds.)

4. Now, bring your attention inward. Reflect on the truth that you are inherently valuable, exactly as you are. Notice if any thoughts or judgments arise, and gently observe them. These thoughts do not define your worth. Your truth is that you are enough, just as you are.

5. (Pause for 1-1.5 minutes to let this settle.)

6. Think about something you appreciate about yourself—something that is uniquely yours. It might be a strength, a talent, or a simple act of kindness you've offered to others. Let that feeling of appreciation expand within you. You have the ability to bring a positive impact to the world simply by being yourself.

7. (Pause for 1.5 minutes for inward reflection.)

8. As you breathe, let each inhale serve as a reminder of your worth. You do not need to seek validation from others to recognize your value. You are inherently worthy. With each exhale, release any doubt or self-criticism that doesn't serve you. This moment is for you to embrace your true potential.

9. (Pause for 1-1.5 minutes.)

10. Gently repeat to yourself: "I am capable. I am worthy. I honor my abilities, just as I am." Let these words settle into your being, each repetition reinforcing your sense of confidence and self-worth.

11. (Pause for 1-1.5 minutes of silent repetition.)

12. When you're ready, slowly bring your awareness back to the present. Know that you can return to this feeling of strength and confidence at any time. You are worthy of respect and recognition, both from others and from yourself. Carry this truth with you as you continue your day.

Script #101: Building Confidence Through Inner Strength

1. Begin by allowing your body to settle comfortably. Feel the weight of your body against the surface you're resting on. Notice the rhythm of your breath, steady and natural. There's no rush here. Just breathe and be present.

2. (Pause for 45-60 seconds.)

3. Think about the person you are, beyond your roles, beyond the expectations. Take a moment to simply acknowledge your true essence. There is no need for comparison or judgment. You are enough, exactly as you are.

4. (Pause for 45-60 seconds to reflect.)

5. With each breath, invite a sense of confidence to rise within you. You are not defined by the mistakes you've made or the flaws you believe you have. You are whole, exactly as you are. In this moment, you are allowed to be yourself, free from any need for approval.

6. (Pause for 1-1.5 minutes.)

7. Now, repeat these words gently or in your mind to yourself, with conviction: "I trust in myself. I am capable of facing anything that comes my way. My confidence grows from within." Feel the truth of these words resonate within your body. Confidence does not come from external validation—it is rooted in your own belief in your strength and abilities.

8. (Pause for 30-45 seconds.)

9. Notice how your body feels as you repeat these affirmations. What shifts? How does your energy feel? Let that sensation grow, knowing that with each repetition, you are reinforcing your belief in yourself and your potential.

10. (Pause for another 30-45 seconds.)

11. As you finish this practice, take a deep breath and carry this feeling of strength and assurance with you. Confidence is not something you need to seek—it is something that you can cultivate by embracing your own abilities. You have all that you need to face life with power and grace. When you're ready, gently open your eyes, knowing that you are capable, worthy, and confident.

Final Thoughts

In this chapter, we've explored how crafting and working with scripts with intentional themes can transform meditation practices. Understanding the nuances of intention setting means that you can help those you work with ground their thoughts, manage stress, and foster personal growth. As we've seen, different themes—be it seasonal, environmental, or spiritual—serve specific needs, offering personalized journeys for each participant.

Conclusion

As we wrap up this exploration into the role of mindfulness and meditation in holistic practices, it's clear that these tools are more than just trends—they are incredible methods for enhancing well-being and addressing the diverse concerns of those you work with. For yoga instructors, life coaches, therapists, counselors, and other wellness practitioners, integrating mindfulness into your practice not only supports your clients' growth but also benefits your own personal and professional experience.

Incorporating these meditation scripts into your sessions can promote holistic benefits, helping clients build a mindset of self-compassion, develop emotional resilience, and enhance their overall well-being. Whether you're working with individuals or groups, these practices will support clients as they face life's challenges with confidence and strength. And as you continue to share these tools, you'll find that they also deepen your own understanding of mindfulness, connection, and personal growth.

Keep in mind that all great things take time. While these practices are designed to encourage healing and growth, patience and consistency are necessary. Be gentle with your clients as they explore these exercises and honor their unique pace. The growth they seek will unfold as they gradually connect more deeply with themselves, and your role as a guide will be invaluable in supporting that process.

Ultimately, the goal is to create experiences that resonate deeply and authentically. Embrace the power of these meditation practices, knowing that by guiding others through these meaningful moments, you are contributing to healing, growth, and lasting positive change. Your presence, your voice, and your intention all matter. As you continue on this path, remain open, patient, and compassionate, trusting that each step forward—no matter how small—brings you and those you serve closer to a deeper sense of connection, peace, and transformation. The journey is ongoing, and your dedication is a vital part of that unfolding.

Thank You for Being Here

I truly hope this book brought value to your journey and offered moments of insight or inspiration along the way. If it resonated with you, I'd be grateful if you took a moment to share your thoughts in a review on Amazon.

Your feedback not only supports the work—it also helps future readers decide if this book is right for them.

Thank you again for your time and support.

References

Ackerman, C. (2017, January 18). *22 mindfulness exercises, techniques &* *activities* *for* *adults.* PositivePsychology.com. https://positivepsychology.com/mindfulness-exercises-techniques-activities/

Agents of Change. (2025, February 12). *Advanced techniques for fostering resilience in clients through therapy.* Agents of Change Social Work Test Prep. https://agentsofchangeprep.com/blog/advanced-techniques-for-fostering-resilience-in-clients-through-therapy/

Archer, A. (n.d.). Self-care while grieving: 10 coping strategies. *Eterneva.* https://www.eterneva.com/resources/self-care-while-grieving

Balban, M. Y., Neri, E., Kogon, M. M., Weed, L., Nouriani, B., Jo, B., Holl, G., Zeitzer, J. M., Spiegel, D., & Huberman, A. D. (2023, January 10). Brief structured respiration practices enhance mood and reduce physiological arousal. *Cell Reports Medicine,* 4(1), 1000895. https://doi.org/10.1016/j.xcrm.2022.100895

Beer, J. (2023, October 10). *6 best diaphragmatic breathing exercises to reduce anxiety.* PositivePsychology. https://positivepsychology.com/diaphragmatic-breathing/

Bournewood Staff. (2023, October 27). The transformative power of gratitude for good mental health. *Bournewood Health Systems.* https://www.bournewood.com/resources/blog/the-transformative-power-of-gratitude-for-good-mental-health/

Breath meditation: A great way to relieve stress. (2014, April 15). Harvard Health. https://www.health.harvard.edu/mind-and-mood/breath-meditation-a-great-way-to-relieve-stress

Cervantes, C. (2024, July 9). Focus meditation: How to improve your concentration. *tm.* https://www.tm.org/en-us/blog/focus-benefits

Chowdhury, M. R. (2019, April 9). *The neuroscience of gratitude and effects on the brain.* PositivePsychology.com. https://positivepsychology.com/neuroscience-of-gratitude/

Conway, S.-M. (2025, March 30). *200+ heart chakra affirmations: a path to emotional healing and love.* Mindfulness Exercises. https://mindfulnessexercises.com/heart-chakra-affirmations/

Cronkleton, E. (2024, May 17). *10 breathing exercises to try when you're feeling stressed.* Healthline. https://www.healthline.com/health/breathing-exercise

Department of Health & Human Services. (2015, September 30). *Breathing to reduce stress.* BetterHealth. https://www.betterhealth.vic.gov.au/health/healthyliving/breathing-to-reduce-stress

Doll, K. (2019, March 23). *23 resilience building tools and exercises.* PositivePsychology. https://positivepsychology.com/resilience-activities-exercises/

11 guided meditation techniques for anxiety relief. (2024, December 23). Elephant in the Room. https://www.elephantintheroomllc.com/11-guided-meditation-techniques-for-anxiety-relief/

Fargo, S. (2024, February 5). *6 guided group meditation scripts.* Mindfulness Exercises. https://mindfulnessexercises.com/guided-meditation-scripts-for-groups/

Fell, A. (2013, March 27). *Mindfulness from meditation associated with lower stress hormone.* UC Davis. https://www.ucdavis.edu/news/mindfulness-meditation-associated-lower-stress-hormone

Fincham, G. W., Strauss, C., Montero-Marin, J., & Cavanagh, K. (2023, January 9). Effect of breathwork on stress and mental health: A meta-analysis of randomised-controlled trials. *Scientific Reports.* https://doi.org/10.1038/s41598-022-27247-y

42 fun ideas for DBT group activities. (2024, February 10). https://www.mentalhealthness.com/dbt-group-activities/

Fowler, P. (2024, March 5). *Breathing techniques for stress relief.* WebMD. https://www.webmd.com/balance/stress-management/stress-relief-breathing-techniques

gillian. (2022, April 25). *The importance of intention setting* Gillian Dagliesh Therapies. https://www.gilliandalgliesh.com/the-importance-of-intention-setting/

Goldsby, T. L., Goldsby, M. E., McWalters, M., & Mills, P. J. (2016, September 30). Effects of singing bowl sound meditation on mood, tension, and well-being: An Observational Study. *Journal of Evidence-Based Complementary & Alternative Medicine.* https://doi.org/10.1177/2156587216668109

Gotter, A. (2024, September 30). *What Is the 4-7-8 breathing technique?* Healthline; Healthline Media. https://www.healthline.com/health/4-7-8-breathing

Groh, K. (2024, Jan 18). Instant manifestation techniques you'll want to try. *Kenz Groh Coaching.* https://www.kenzgrohcoaching.com/blog/instant-manifestation-techniques-you-ll-want-to-try

Grounding techniques for effective anxiety and stress relief. (2024, March 26). Resilience Lab. https://www.resiliencelab.us/thought-lab/grounding-techniques

Guerra, E. (2024, April 12). *Meditation for productivity: My journey & 3 beginner techniques to focus better.* The Productivity Flow. https://theproductivityflow.com/meditation-productivity-my-journey-3-beginner-techniques-focus-better/

Ho, T. (2023, January 31). *How to set intention as part of your spiritual practice.* Museflower Retreat & Spa.

https://musefloweretreat.com/how-to-set-intention-as-part-of-your-spiritual-practice/

Hölzel, B. K., Carmody, J., Vangel, M., Congleton, C., Yerramsetti, S. M., Gard, T., & Lazar, S. W. (2011). Mindfulness practice leads to increases in regional brain gray matter density. *Psychiatry Research: Neuroimaging, 191*(1), 36–43. https://doi.org/10.1016/j.pscychresns.2010.08.006

How to practice breath meditation to relieve stress. (n.d.). *Calm Blog.* https://www.calm.com/blog/breath-meditation

Incorporating mindfulness techniques in your daily routine. (n.d.). Life Coach Certification Online. https://lifecoachtraining.co/incorporating-mindfulness-techniques-in-your-daily-routine/

Insight Timer Editorial Team. (2024, December 17). Releasing meditation: Let go of the past and embrace your power. *Insight Timer Blog.* https://insighttimer.com/blog/insighttimer-com-blog-releasing-meditation-inner-witch/

Keng, S. L., Smoski, M. J., & Robins, C. J. (2011). Effects of mindfulness on psychological health: A review of empirical studies. *Clinical Psychology Review, 31*(6), 1041-1056. https://doi.org/10.1016/j.cpr.2011.04.006

Kriakous, S. A., Elliott, K. A., Lamers, C., & Owen, R. (2021). The effectiveness of mindfulness-based stress reduction on the psychological functioning of healthcare professionals: a systematic review. *Mindfulness, 12*(1), 1–28. https://doi.org/10.1007/s12671-020-01500-9

Life Coach Magazine. (2025). *5, 10, and 15-minute guided morning meditation scripts.* Life Coach Magazine. https://www.lifecoachmagazine.com/morning-meditation-script/

Majsiak, B., & Young, C. (2022, June 23). *7 ways to practice breath work for beginners.* Everyday Health.

https://www.everydayhealth.com/alternative-health/living-with/ways-practice-breath-focused-meditation/

Mayo Clinic Staff. (2022, October 11). *Mindfulness exercises*. Mayo Clinic. https://www.mayoclinic.org/healthy-lifestyle/consumer-health/in-depth/mindfulness-exercises/art-20046356

McCraty, R., & Zayas, M. A. (2014, September 29). Cardiac coherence, self-regulation, autonomic stability, and psychosocial well-being. *Frontiers in Psychology*. https://doi.org/10.3389/fpsyg.2014.01090

Meditative journey: Storytelling in guided meditation. (2023, November 18). *The Mind Orchestra*. https://www.themindorchestra.com/blog/meditative-guided-meditation-storytelling

Mindful Staff. (2020, July 8). *What is mindfulness?* Mindful. https://www.mindful.org/what-is-mindfulness/

Mindfulness therapy: The power of living in the moment. (2024, March 5). *Sierra Vista Hospital*. https://sierravistahospital.com/blog/mindfulness-therapy-the-power-of-living-in-the-moment/

Nash, J. (2025, January 14). *25 self-reflection questions: Why introspection is important*. PositivePsychology.com. https://positivepsychology.com/introspection-self-reflection/

Neff, K. (2024). *Self-compassion practices*. Self-Compassion. https://self-compassion.org/self-compassion-practices/

Nguyen, J., & Brymer, E. (2018, October 2). Nature-based guided imagery as an Iitervention for state anxiety. *Frontiers in Psychology*. https://doi.org/10.3389/fpsyg.2018.01858

Parker, C. (2025, January 19). *Addressing 10 common myths about meditation*. Light Warriors Legion. https://lightwarriorslegion.com/addressing-common-myths-about-meditation/

Paszkiel, S., Dobrakowski, P., & Łysiak, A. (2020). The impact of different sounds on stress level in the context of EEG, cardiac measures and subjective stress level: A pilot study. *Brain Sciences*, *10*(10), 728. https://doi.org/10.3390/brainsci10100728

Sahu, B. (2024, November 23). *Rise and shine: Morning rituals for a brighter mind.* Medium; ILLUMINATION. https://medium.com/illumination/rise-and-shine-morning-rituals-for-a-brighter-mind-8c45fd979ef0

Schumacher, G. (2024, February 27). The power of emotional intelligence. *South University.* https://www.southuniversity.edu/news-and-blogs/2024/02/the-power-of-emotional-intelligence

Sinha, R. (2024, November 6). *101 ways to mindfulness and meditation practices for live healthy lifestyle in 2024.* Medium. https://medium.com/@ratneshwarprasadsinha_66909/101-ways-to-mindfulness-and-meditation-practices-for-live-healthy-lifestyle-in-2024-04d860cfd51c

Smith, K. (2019, May 7). *10 ways to incorporate meditation into your yoga practice.* Beyogi. https://beyogi.com/ways-to-incorporate-meditation-into-your-yoga-practice/

Stuarttan. (2024, July 15) *Timeline therapy: transforming past experiences into career strengths.* https://www.stuarttan.com/timeline-therapy-transforming-past-experiences-into-career-strengths/

Sutton, J. (2022, February 12). *Visualization in therapy: 16 simple techniques & tools.* Positive Psychology. https://positivepsychology.com/visualization-techniques/

Team Simply.Coach. (2024, November 14). Incorporating mindfulness into your coaching practice: A focus on wellness. *Simply.Coach.* https://simply.coach/blog/coaching-and-mindfulness-in-practice/

Telford, S. (2023, September 19). Embracing the seasons: Integrating the seasons into yoga classes. *Medium.*

https://sallylouisetelford.medium.com/embracing-the-seasons-integrating-the-seasons-into-yoga-classes-23ef12bbf725

Uwumarogie, V. (2022, May 20). *Why honoring grief is a radical and necessary act of self-care.* Essence. https://www.essence.com/lifestyle/grief-as-self-care/

Vandervort, S. (2025, February 8). Cultivating self-love: A guided meditation for inner peace and acceptance. *Okoliving.* https://okoliving.com/blogs/home/self-love-meditation?srsltid=AfmBOoqaA7GvJxhkeBt5eHqlKK3wS48w KAstjYNG0AyXZew10Aoikma_

West, M. (2022, April 21). *What to know about guided imagery.* Medical News Today. https://www.medicalnewstoday.com/articles/guided-imagery

Woliba Marketing Team. (2024, April 9). 10 spiritual wellness activities to connect with your inner self. *Woliba.* https://woliba.io/blog/spiritual-wellness-activities/

Your Headspace Mindfulness & Meditation Experts. (2023, Januray 20). *Breating exercises to reduce stress.* Headspace. https://www.headspace.com/meditation/breathing-exercises

Made in United States
Cleveland, OH
24 June 2025

17962107R00134